little birds

26 Handmade Projects to Sew, Stitch, Quilt & Love

Compiled by Susanne Woods

stash
an imprint of C&T Publishing

Text and artwork copyright © 2010 by C&T Publishing, Inc.

Publisher: Amy Marson

Creative Director: Gailen Runge

Acquisitions Editor: Susanne Woods

Editors: Cynthia Bix and Ann Haley

Technical Editor: Ann Haley

Photography by Christina Carty-Francis
and Diane Pedersen of C&T Publishing, Inc.,
unless otherwise noted

Copyeditor/Proofreader: Wordfirm Inc.

Design Direction: Kristy Zacharias

Cover/Book Designer: Kerry Graham

Production Coordinator: Zinnia Heinzmann

Production Editor: Julia Cianci

Illustrator: Tim Manibusan

Published by Stash an imprint of C&T Publishing, Inc., P.O. Box 1456, Lafayette, CA 94549

Library of Congress Cataloging-in-Publication Data

Little birds : 26 handmade projects to sew, stitch, quilt & love.

   p. cm.

ISBN 978-1-60705-003-2 (soft cover)

1. Handicraft. 2. Machine sewing. 3. Birds in art. I. C&T Publishing.

TT157.L52 2010

745.5--dc22

2009043746

Printed in China

10 9 8 7 6 5 4 3 2 1

contents

introduction

Like many of you who have picked up this book, I have a love of fabric and sewing that goes back more years than I care to remember. When my passion became my career in my role as the Acquisitions Editor for Stash, the most time-consuming (and the most enviable) aspect of my work became searching for talented individuals and inviting them to write books for us.

I am constantly looking for inspiration and drooling over the exciting creations I have seen in magazines, at craft fairs, and all over the Internet. Over time, I have seen my share of the odd and irregular (and just plain weird), but what I long for is a stunning project that is beautiful and sweet—perfect for gifting, decorating, or displaying. And then I started seeing the most amazing birds take form at the hands of some truly awesome fabric artists.

This book represents the work of some of these designers and showcases projects they have created featuring their birds. This is the first book in a series of titles called Design Collective. In this series, I have invited a group of clever artists who have taken pieces of cloth or yarn to amazing levels and have asked them to share one of their most loved projects in our book. Within these pages you will find quilts, soft sculpture, embroidery, and even a bit of knitting!

All of these projects will make you feel like an artist and will inspire you to learn new skills and work with a variety of materials. Each includes detailed step-by-step instructions so that you can create the project just as the designer did, or you can take off on your own flight of fancy. Some of the projects are simple, and some a bit more of a challenge, but all are whimsical, handsome, lovely little creations. I hope you enjoy making this entire flock of little birds.

Susanne Woods

Little Birds Mobile

FINISHED SIZE OF BIRDS: 6½″ × 3″ × 2″

Dangle these little birds from a wreath as shown here, or prop them on a branch and hang it on a wall. One bird can nest in the wreath. You can also use the birds individually as pincushions or decorations.

ARTIST **EMAIL**
Bari J. Ackerman Bari@barijonline.com

WEBSITES
www.barijonline.com
www.barij.typepad.com (blog)

Bari is a product/textile designer and owner of Bari J. designs, based in the San Francisco Bay Area. To date, she has created two fabric lines for Windham Fabrics—Full Bloom and Art Journal. She is currently working on a book for C&T Publishing.

MATERIALS AND CUTTING INSTRUCTIONS

Patterns are on page 101. Make 8 birds.

Fabric scraps in several prints and colors, each at least 8″ × 3″, for the bird bodies, gussets, and wings:

- Cut 16 bird bodies (8 and 8 reversed).
- Cut 8 gussets.

½ yard fusible woven cotton interfacing such as Form Flex for the bird body:

- Cut 16 bird bodies of interfacing (8 and 8 reversed).
- Cut 8 gussets of interfacing.

Polyester batting or fiberfill for stuffing

6″ × 6″ piece of muslin or scrap fabric for the nest

Double-sided fusible web for the wings

Wire for the bird wings

Faux branches and leaves, or a pretty wreath

Doll-maker's needle

Spray starch

Yarn in several colors to hang the birds

MAKE THE BIRDS

1. Follow the manufacturer's directions to attach interfacing to the wrong side of each bird body and gusset.

2. Using a pencil, mark each tip of the gusset at ¼", as indicated on the pattern. This will be where you stop and start sewing.

3. Place the gusset on top of the bird, right sides together along the belly of the bird, as shown in Figure 1 below. *Note: You'll sew one-half of the gusset to one bird body, and then sew the other half to a reversed bird body.*

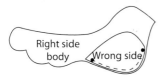

Figure 1

4. Starting at one of the dots, sew a ¼" seam to the other dot, backstitching at each end.

5. Fold the gusset down, and place the other bird body on it, lining it up along the belly of the bird, right sides together, as shown in

Figure 2. Attach the second half of the gusset to the second body of the bird with a ¼" seam. Start where you stopped sewing the other half of the gusset and stop where you started sewing, backstitching at each end.

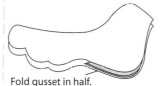

Fold gusset in half.
Figure 2

Sew the two halves of the bird together

1. Leaving a 2" gap in the top of the tail, sew a ¼" seam from one corner of the gusset to the other, backstitching at each end.

2. Turn the bird right side out through the opening you left.

3. Stuff well with batting or fiberfill. It's helpful to use the end of a paintbrush to pull the tail through all the way and to stuff the tail. Slipstitch the opening shut.

Make the wings

1. Using the wing pattern, trace 16 wings (8 and 8 reversed) onto the right side of a piece of fabric with chalk or an erasable sewing marker.

2. Mark a line on the wrong side of the fabric to indicate where you traced the wings so that you can see where to place the wire.

3. Fold a 4" piece of wire in half, and then bend in the ends. Wrap the wire with tape (any kind of tape will do) so that it does not poke through the fabric.

4. Place the wire along the middle of the wing, between the wrong sides of the piece that you just traced and another piece of fabric. Using double-sided fusible web, fuse the 2 pieces of fabric together.

5. Cut the wings out along chalk lines.

6. Using a zigzag stitch, sew around the wing that you drew in chalk.

7. Center your needle over one end of the piece of wire, and zigzag stitch over it to hold the wire in place.

8. Either glue (using a fabric glue such as Fabri-Tac) or hand stitch the wings in place, using the project photo as a guide.

String the birds for hanging

1. Thread the doll-maker's needle with a piece of yarn. (Vary the length for each bird to make a dynamic-looking mobile.) Double the knot at the end of the yarn.

2. From the front of the gusset, poke the needle through to the top at an angle heading toward the back of the bird. This allows the bird to hang without tilting.

MAKE THE NEST

1. Being very careful not to cut yourself, use a rotary cutter to shred a pile of fabric scraps. You'll want to end up with about 2 cups full.

2. Create an oval piece of muslin about 6″ long by 5″ wide.

3. Place the muslin oval under the needle on your sewing machine. Place a chunk of scraps on top of the muslin.

4. Sew back and forth and around and around until the scraps are "nailed down."

5. Flip the piece, shake off the excess, and fill any holes.

6. Repeat on the other side.

7. Wet the piece, wring it out, and allow the nest to dry.

8. Spray thoroughly with spray starch, and, using your iron, bend up the edges to make a nest-like shape.

9. Spray again with starch, and allow to dry.

ASSEMBLE THE MOBILE

1. Create a wreath shape with faux branches and leaves, and wire the ends together.

2. Hang the birds at varying lengths from the wreath.

3. Attach yarn or wire to hang the wreath.

4. Lay the nest in place on top of the wreath, and add a bird.

Fancy Peacock

FINISHED SIZE: ABOUT 8″ × 7″ × 6″

What's not to be proud of when you look this fabulous? Combine wool felt, unique buttons, and creative hand embroidery to create this tactile peacock who displays well no matter where he sits.

ARTIST
Amy Adams

EMAIL
lucykatecrafts@talktalk.net

WEBSITES
www.lucykatecrafts.etsy.com
www.folksy.com/shops/lucykatecrafts/
www.lucykatecrafts.blogspot.com (blog)

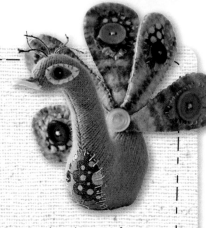

Amy Adams is a UK-based textile artist specializing in designing and making softies from an ever-increasing catalog of patterns. These softies are available as one-off pieces and also as published patterns. Her work mixes vintage and recycled fabrics and felted wool, with a dash of hand-stitched embroidery.

MATERIALS AND CUTTING INSTRUCTIONS

Patterns are on page 101.

6″ × 12″ prefelted wool for the body:
- Cut 2 body pieces (make sure that if the wool has a right side and a wrong side, one body shape is cut in reverse from the other).

3″ × 6″ printed fabric for the tummy:
- Cut 1 tummy piece.

2″ × 3″ cream felt for the eyes and beak:
- Cut 2 outer eye shapes and 2 beak shapes.

2″ × 2″ turquoise felt for the eyes and beak:
- Cut 2 inner eye shapes and 1 inner beak shape.

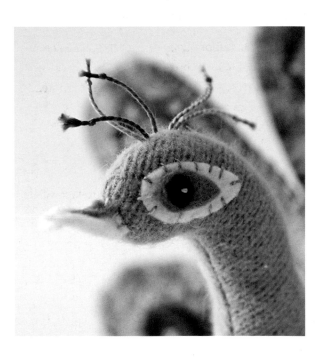

12″ × 5″ prefelted wool (to coordinate with the body) for the front of the tail:

- Cut 5 of tail Template 1.

3 pieces 4″ × 5″ coordinating printed fabrics for the back of the tail feathers:

- Cut 5 of tail Template 1 (use the prints randomly).

10″ × 3″ printed fabric for the eye of the tail feathers:

- Cut 5 of tail Template 2.

10″ × 5″ thin cardboard for stiffening the tail:

- Cut 5 of tail Template 3.

Embroidery floss (Use perle cotton #8 for all the main stitching and perle cotton #5 for the head plume.)

Wool batting or fiberfill for stuffing

Small pebbles (approximately 3) to weight the body (The body will need some weight to it in order for it to stand up. You can use dried rice or lentils instead of pebbles if you wish.)

2 small buttons for the eyes

6 large buttons for the tail

A stuffer stick (A knitting needle or chopstick will do!)

Tip

The 6 larger buttons do not need to match. You can use any from your stash or from old clothes. If you can't find small buttons to use for the eyes, just stitch on small circles of dark-colored felt instead.

CONSTRUCTION

Note: The body can be sewn either by hand using a backstitch (see page 111) or on a sewing machine.

1. Pin the 2 body pieces, right sides together, and sew around the edge, leaving a 1½″ gap across the base.

2. Turn the body right side out, using the stuffer stick to poke out the head. Begin to stuff, remembering to place 2 or 3 pebbles wrapped in some additional stuffing within the tummy base. The body needs to be heavier than you would think to counterbalance the tail. As you are stuffing, wiggle the body shape around to make sure it is smooth, with no odd lumps or bumps.

3. Place the wider end of the tummy piece over the open gap so that the narrower end lies over the chest area. Fix it in place with some small, random straight stitches, using the embroidery floss.

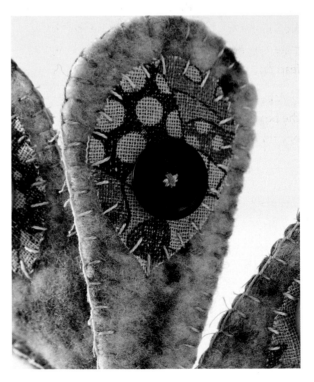

4. Position the cream felt eye shape to one side of the peacock's head, and attach it with more random straight stitches. Place the turquoise eye piece on top, and secure it by stitching on a small button. Do the same to the other side of the head.

5. Sandwich the 3 layers of the beak (2 pieces of cream felt and the smaller piece of turquoise felt) together, and join them using a running stitch down the center of the beak. Anchor the beak to the head as shown.

6. Add the head plumage threads using the thicker embroidery floss (use perle cotton #5). Cut a length of 8″ (20cm), sew it through the top of the head, unthread it from the needle, and tie a knot to each end, 1″ from the head. Trim each length just above the knot. Repeat this process twice more.

7. Taking 1 wool felt tail feather at a time, stitch on the fabric feather eye (tail template 2) using random straight stitches, and then add a button.

8. Lay out the tail feather pieces on a tabletop, and match up each feather by layering 1 piece of prefelted wool with a fabric backing. Place 1 piece of the cardboard between the felt and the fabric, and sew around the edge of both using a blanket stitch (see page 111). Repeat this process for the remaining 4 feathers.

9. Attach the feathers, one at a time in a fan shape, to the peacock's tail. Finish it off by adding another large button in the center to hide your stitching.

Stork with a Heart Mobile

FINISHED SIZE OF STORK: ABOUT 10″ × 6″ × 2½″

This sweet mobile for a new baby features a heart dangling from the stork's beak. You can personalize it by embroidering the heart with the baby's name and birth date.

ARTIST
Amy Adams

EMAIL
lucykatecrafts@talktalk.net

WEBSITES
www.lucykatecrafts.etsy.com
www.folksy.com/shops/lucykatecrafts/
www.lucykatecrafts.blogspot.com (blog)

MATERIALS AND CUTTING INSTRUCTIONS

Patterns are on page 102.

8" × 12" prefelted wool (white or cream) for the body and heart:

- Cut 2 body shapes from the prefelted wool, making sure that one body shape is cut in reverse from the other if the wool has a right side and a wrong side.
- Cut 1 heart shape.

4" × 17" printed fabric for the tummy, wings, tail, and heart:

- Cut 1 tummy shape.
- Cut 2 wings (1 and 1 reversed).
- Cut 1 tail.
- Cut 1 heart.

2" × 2" white felt for the eyes:

- Cut 2 eyes.

4" × 16" prefelted brown wool for the beak, wings, and tail:

- Cut 1 inner beak.
- Cut 2 wings (1 and 1 reversed).
- Cut 1 tail.

2" × 3" yellow felt for the beak:

- Cut 2 outer beaks.

1 large button for the heart

Felt circle (slightly larger than the button) for the heart

Wool batting or fiberfill for stuffing

Embroidery floss (Use perle cotton #8.)

2 small buttons for the eyes

2 large buttons for the feet

12" length of yellow wool yarn for the legs

A stuffer stick such as a knitting needle or chopstick.

MAKE THE STORK

See page 111 for embroidery stitches.

1. Pin the 2 body pieces right sides together, and sew around the edge, leaving a 1½" gap across the tummy. Turn the body right side out, using the stuffer stick to poke out the head. Begin to stuff, and, as you go, wiggle around the body shape to make sure it is smooth, with no odd lumps or bumps.

2. Place the tummy fabric over the opening, and fix it into position using random straight stitches. Add an eye to one side of the stork's head by stitching a small button centrally on top of a white felt disc; repeat for the other eye.

3. Next, sandwich the 3 layers of the beak together (2 pieces of the yellow felt and a smaller piece of the brown felt), and join them with a running stitch down the center, using the embroidery floss. Slipstitch the beak in position on the stork's head.

4. Construct the wings by placing the prefelted wool and the printed fabric wrong sides together, and pin. Repeat for the other wing, which is the reverse of the first wing. Sew around each wing with a blanket stitch, using the embroidery floss; leave the joining edge blank. Make the tail in the same way, except this time you need to make only one.

5. Using a running stitch, attach the 2 wings and tail onto the stork's body, fabric side up, first by catching the fabric with each stitch. Then turn the bird over, and do the same with the felted layer underneath.

6. Add the legs by threading a needle with the length of yellow wool yarn. Sew each loose end of wool yarn through a button, and secure with a knot at the bottom to fix on each button foot.

MAKE THE HEART

To make the birth-date heart, embroider the pre-felted wool with the name and date, either by hand, using embroidery floss and the back-stitch, or using free-motion machine embroidery. Place the embroidered wool heart wrong sides together with the patterned fabric heart, and stitch around the edge with a blanket stitch. Add a little decoration by attaching a circle of colored felt with a button on top.

ASSEMBLE THE MOBILE

Stitch one end of a 12″ length of embroidery floss to the stork's back, centrally between the wings, and tie the other end in a loop for hanging. Stitch one end of another length of floss to the heart, and the other through the beak; tie on with a knot. Hold the mobile up to double-check the hanging thread lengths, and adjust if required.

Our Flock Embroidery

FINISHED STITCHERY SIZE: 8½″ × 4″

Celebrate your own family flock with an embroidery project perfect for personalizing.

ARTIST
Heidi Allred

EMAIL
frontstreetdesigns@yahoo.com

WEBSITES
www.frontstreetstitching.com
www.frontstreetdesigns.etsy.com (shop)
www.frontstreetdesigns.blogspot.com (blog)

Heidi Allred started Front Street Designs LLC in January 2009. "I had a hard time finding patterns that I loved, so I decided to draw my own!" Heidi started selling online, and in the fall of 2009 began selling in stores.

MATERIALS AND SUPPLIES

DMC FLOSS 581, 604, 712, 899, 3348, 3752, 3753, 3781 (Feel free to get creative with the colors of DMC floss. Use colors to match your décor, or your kids' personalities.)

11″ × 9″ muslin (predyed, or you can tea dye it yourself when the stitchery is complete)

11″ × 9″ Warm & Natural batting

Frame with cardboard insert

TRACING THE PATTERN

The pattern is on page 101. See page 111 for embroidery stitches.

Tape the pattern to a sunny window or a lightbox. Center the muslin over the pattern, and trace with a pencil or water-erasable fabric pen. If you use a pencil, be careful. You'll have to be precise and be sure to cover every mark when stitching. The pencil isn't easy to remove. This pattern is a custom pattern. Be sure to add as many birds as needed to match the members of your family. Just use the pattern and line up the birds on the branch. Feel free to leave off any of the top little twigs to fit more birds on the branch. When the tracing is done, place the muslin over the Warm & Natural batting, and stitch through both layers. This helps hide the threads and gives your finished piece some body.

STITCHING

Use 3 strands of floss unless otherwise indicated. Most stitches will be made using a backstitch. French knots will be used when indicated.

3781 BROWN. Stitch the brackets and branch. Stitch all the birds' eyes, beaks, and legs, and the bows on the girl birds (all using 2 strands). Stitch the words "Our Flock" (2 strands). For the center of the bows, tie a French knot.

3752 DARKER BLUE. Stitch the largest boy bird.

3753 LIGHTER BLUE. Stitch the smaller boy bird(s).

899 DARKER PINK. Stitch the largest girl bird.

604 LIGHTER PINK. Stitch the smaller girl bird(s). Tie random French knots around the leaves and twigs.

581 DARKER GREEN. Stitch 8 random leaves.

3348 LIGHTER GREEN. Stitch the 6 remaining leaves.

712 CREAMY WHITE. Tie additional French knots around the leaves and twigs.

FINISHING

If you are using a water-erasable pen, quickly rinse the entire stitchery with water. Lay out to dry. For quicker drying, iron on a medium/hot setting. When the piece is completely dry, iron it again. If you are framing the stitchery, center it on stiff cardboard cut to the frame size. Wrap the edges around the cardboard, and tape them on the back. Be sure to pull the muslin taught so it lies flat on the front. Frame and enjoy your new piece of artwork!

Our Flock

Tips on tea dyeing

Mix 1–2 Tbsp. of instant tea (I use Lipton) in 1 cup warm water. Lay the finished stitchery on a foil-lined cookie sheet, and apply the tea with a foam brush. Saturate the muslin completely. For darker areas, let some tea puddle in spots on the muslin. Let dry in a 200° oven. Remember that all muslins dye differently.

Tweet Birds
Apron

FINISHED STITCHERY SIZE: 8″ × 8″

Could these lovebirds be carving their initials in the tree? Either way, this pair will make perfect partners in the kitchen, embroidered on this stylish apron.

ARTIST
Heidi Allred

EMAIL
frontstreetdesigns@yahoo.com

WEBSITES
www.frontstreetstitching.com
www.frontstreetdesigns.etsy.com (shop)
www.frontstreetdesigns.blogspot.com (blog)

MATERIALS AND SUPPLIES

DMC FLOSS: 504, 712, 734, 3781, 3853 (Feel free to get creative with the colors of DMC floss.)

10″ × 10″ muslin (predyed, or you can tea dye it yourself when the stitchery is complete)

10″ × 10″ Warm & Natural batting

Optional: Ready-made apron or pillowcase (It may be easier to stitch the embroidery on muslin first and then add it to an apron or pillowcase—or make your own!)

TRACING THE PATTERN

The pattern is on page 102. Refer to page 20 for tips on tracing the pattern.

STITCHING

Use 3 strands of floss unless otherwise indicated. Most stitches will be made using a backstitch. French knots will be used when indicated. See page 111 for embroidery stitches.

3781 BROWN. Stitch the tree trunk. Stitch the birds' legs, beaks, and eyes, and the words "tweet tweet" (using 2 strands). Tie French knots in the center of the first blue flower, on the stem behind the blue bird, and before the words "tweet tweet" (2 strands).

734 GREEN. Stitch the tree and grass. Stitch the flower stems and leaves (2 strands).

504 BLUE. Stitch the smaller bird. Stitch the first and last 3-petal flower, and tie French knots in the center of the flower by the larger bird (2 strands).

3853 ORANGE. Stitch the larger bird. Tie French knots on the small flower by the first 3-petal flower, in the center of the second 3-petal flower, on the stem by the smaller bird, and on the stem at the end of the words "tweet tweet" (2 strands).

712 CREAMY WHITE. Stitch the 3-petal flowers behind the smaller bird and in front of the larger bird, and tie French knots in the last 3-petal flower (2 strands).

TEA DYING

Refer to page 21 for tips on tea dying embroidery.

FINISHING

If you are using a water-erasable pen, quickly rinse the entire stitchery with water. Lay out to dry. For quicker drying, iron on a medium/hot setting. When the piece is completely dry, iron it again.

Add finished embroidery to a ready-made apron or incorporate it into your own creation. The embroidery for this project was sewn into the top of a hand-made apron by adding strips to each of the four sides. The neck strap, ties, and skirt were then added. The top part of the apron is fully lined to hide the back of the embroidery.

Birdhouse

FINISHED BIRDHOUSE SIZE: 7½″ HIGH × 6½″ WIDE × 4″ DEEP

For Rent: One birdhouse, patched roof, impeccable construction, charming neighborhood, a perfect starter home, move-in ready. Bring your own embellishments and make it your own.

ARTIST
Abigail Brown

EMAIL
Abigailbrown81@hotmail.com

WEBSITE
www.abigail-brown.co.uk

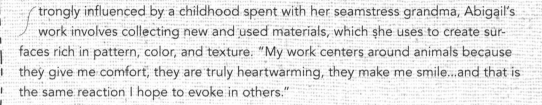

trongly influenced by a childhood spent with her seamstress grandma, Abigail's work involves collecting new and used materials, which she uses to create surfaces rich in pattern, color, and texture. "My work centers around animals because they give me comfort, they are truly heartwarming, they make me smile...and that is the same reaction I hope to evoke in others."

MATERIALS AND SUPPLIES

¼ yard of striped or bold patterned/colored fabric for the roof

1 yard of plain or light-colored/patterned fabric for the birdhouse

1 yard of fusible web

Scraps of different colored and patterned fabrics

Fabric glue

CONSTRUCTION

The pattern is on page 102.

Note: All seam allowances are ½".

House

1. Create a paper birdhouse template using the pattern.

2. Cut 2 pieces of the plain-colored fabric large enough for the house template, and 1 piece of the fusible web to the same size.

3. Sandwich the fusible web between the 2 fabric layers, and press with an iron to fix.

4. Draw around the house template lightly but visibly, and cut leaving a ½" seam allowance on all sides. Cut out the small inner hole.

5. Fold as indicated on the pattern. Pin adjoining sides a to sides b, and sew along the pencil lines to form the 4-sided box.

6. Turn inside out, and press all 4 sides of the box and the 4 edges of the base.

Roof

1. Create a paper roof template using the dimensions below.

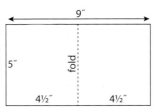

Birdhouse roof

2. Cut 2 birdhouse roof 5" × 9" rectangles from the striped or bright fabric, large enough to fit the roof template, and one the same size from the fusible web. Sandwich the fusible web between the 2 layers of fabric (wrong sides together), and press with an iron to fix.

3. Cut different lengths of the scrap fabrics, and arrange them on the roof, creating a rough look resembling planks of wood. Sew the strips, leaving the ends of the threads loose, approximately ½"–1" long.

4. Fold the roof piece in half, scrap side outward, and press with an iron.

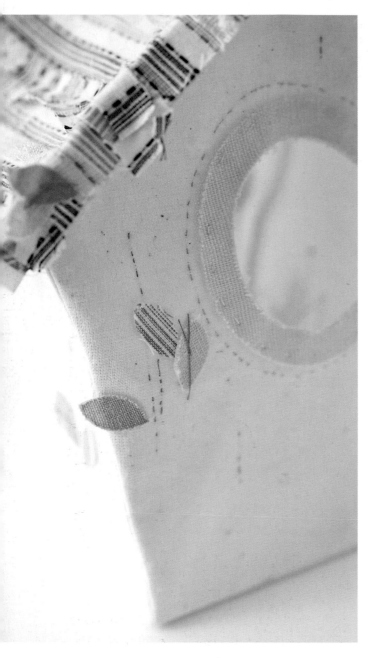

ASSEMBLY

1. Press the 6 top edges of the box along the pencil lines, folding outward to form flaps.

2. Starting from the peak of the front panel of the box, pin on the roof from its center, folded point outward.

3. Hand sew all 6 edges to secure the roof to the box.

4. Create a paper ring template using the circles on the birdhouse pattern on page 102. Using the paper ring template, cut a ring of fabric from the scraps, and attach it around the hole using fabric glue.

5. Cut leaves from the scraps, and arrange them on the house and roof; attach with fabric glue.

6. Hand sew detailing to the birdhouse using tiny vertical running stitches to replicate the wood grain.

Fred the Cardinal

FINISHED SIZE: 5″ × 9½″ × 6″

Quite frankly, when your everyday is everyone else's Sunday best, you're bound to feel a little pleased with yourself. With the clever stitching, flawless construction, and awesome feet, every side is this bird's good side.

ARTIST
Eleanor Bruce

EMAIL
abcdebruce@gmail.com

WEBSITE
www.thequirkycorncrib.etsy.com (shop)

Eleanor Bruce's family loves to design new things with old stuff. "My daughters and I create creatures, mostly owls, out of felt and recycled fabrics." Their creatures are mostly one of a kind, made without patterns. "We'd love to have you visit our shop and see our most recent creations."

MATERIALS AND CUTTING INSTRUCTIONS

⅓ yard red felt for the body, wings, and comb:

- Cut 2 bodies
  (1 and 1 reversed).
- Cut 4 wings
  (2 and 2 reversed).
- Cut 2 combs
  (1 and 1 reversed).

6″ × 6″ black felt for the face patch:

- Cut 1 face patch.

3″ × 3″ orange felt for the beak:

- Cut 1 top part of the beak.
- Cut 1 bottom part of the beak.

Small scraps white felt for the eyes:

- Cut 2 eyes.

¼ cup washed gravel or your choice of weighting material

½″-wide thin fabric strips (cut or torn), totaling 120″ for the feet (can be pieced)

2 pieces green floral wire, each 20″ long

2 small black buttons for the eyes

1 skein white embroidery thread

1 skein black embroidery thread

Fiberfill

Water-soluble fabric marker

CONSTRUCTION

Note: All seam allowances are ¼".

Template preparation

Patterns are on page 103.

1. Trace the patterns, and cut out the templates.

2. Pin the templates, and cut out the fabric pieces.

3. Using the water-soluble fabric marker, mark all appliqué placements and the embroidery pattern.

Body assembly

See page 111 for embroidery stitches.

1. From the wrong side, stitch the darts on the body pieces right sides together. Pin the body pieces together, and stitch leaving an opening at the bottom for turning and stuffing. Reverse, and stuff firmly. At the opening in the bottom, pull apart the stuffing to make a small hole, and fill with gravel. Hand stitch the opening closed.

2. Pinch and pin the tail portion as shown, and stitch.

Pinch tail, and stitch.

3. Pin 2 wing pieces with wrong sides together. Using an embroidery backstitch, follow the markings around the wings, bonding them together. Repeat with the second set of wing pieces, making sure to reverse the wing direction.

4. Pin or hold together the comb pieces, and whipstitch around the marked sides. Pull the open area apart a little way, and pin to the top of the head at the markings. Stitch to the head using a whipstitch. Your stitches will show.

5. Pin the black face patch to the body. Using a felting needle, poke rapidly up and down, over and over, until the whole black piece is welded to the felt underneath. Needle felt around the edge first to hold the piece in place, and remove the pins. (If you prefer, this piece can be appliquéd on with a whipstitch.)

6. Mark the location for the white eye patches, and needle felt them to the body.

7. Chain stitch around the eye patches. Following the pattern along the edge of the black felt, embroider using the backstitch.

8. Pin the beak pieces together, and, with black embroidery thread, stitch them together along the straight edges using the cross-stitch. Stuff the beak firmly with fiberfill, and pin it to the black face patch, attaching it with the whipstitch. Make nostrils with a French knot.

9. Pin the wings to the body, and attach with 5 cross-stitches.

10. Sew on the button eyes.

Foot construction and assembly

1. Using the guide pattern (page 103), form the wire feet. Twist each toe until it is stiff. There will be some excess wire to poke up into the body.

2. Starting at the ankle, wrap the strips of fabric up and down each toe. Leave the excess leg wire bare. Cut off the excess fabric. (Optional: If you are having trouble with the cloth slipping, put touches of hot glue on the wire bit by bit ahead of where you are wrapping.)

3. With the black or white embroidery thread, wrap each toe to secure the fabric to the wire. Make a stitch every 2 wraps of the thread.

4. Poke the excess wire up into the body where indicated on the pattern. Secure the feet to the body with several stitches.

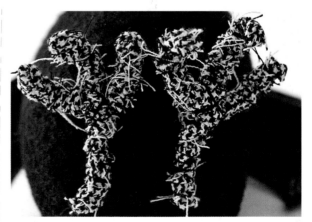

Place feet, and stitch.

5. Bend the toes, balance, and enjoy your masterpiece!

Edward the Owl (and friends)

FINISHED SIZE: 4″ × 6¾″ × 2½″

This dapper posse of professors looks just as ready to start a rock band as they do to star in a Wild West showdown.

ARTIST
Eleanor Bruce

EMAIL
abcdebruce@gmail.com

WEBSITE
www.thequirkycorncrib.etsy.com (shop)

MATERIALS AND CUTTING INSTRUCTIONS

Patterns are on page 104.

9″ × 10″ fabric for the owl body, wings, and tail:
- Cut 2 owl bodies.
- Cut 4 wings.
- Cut 2 tails.

6″ × 6″ fabric for the hips/legs:
- Cut 4 hip/legs.

3″ × 6″ fabric for the square top piece:
- Cut 2 top pieces.

2″ × 10″ fabric for the collar:
- Cut 1 collar.

5″ × 10″ felt for the jacket:
- Cut 1 jacket.

1″ × 2″ felt for the eye patches:
- Cut 2 eye patches.

1 felting needle

4 pieces fabric for wrapping the legs, each approximately ½″ × 48″

2 small pinches of boa feathers for the ear tufts

1 button approximately ¾″–1″ in diameter for the jacket

2 small black buttons for the eyes

6″ of ¼″-wide ribbon for the bowtie

Fiberfill for stuffing

Gold or pumpkin-colored embroidery thread for the beak

1 skein embroidery thread to coordinate with the owl colors

2 pieces medium-weight floral wire, each 22″ long

Water-soluble fabric marker

Optional: Hot glue, fabric glue, knitting needle

CONSTRUCTION

Template preparation

1. Trace the pattern pieces, and make the templates for cutting.

2. Pin the templates, and cut the fabric pieces.

3. With the water-soluble fabric pen, transfer all the placement marks to the cut fabric pieces.

Body assembly

Note: All seam allowances are ¼". See page 111 for embroidery stitches.

1. Stitch with right sides together where indicated on the body, wing, tail, and hip/leg pieces.

2. Turn all the pieces inside out. Stitch the square top piece all the way around. Cut a small slit in the middle of one side, and turn inside out.

3. Firmly stuff the body, and stitch closed. Stuff the hip/leg pieces, but do not stitch closed.

Leg assembly

1. Following the foot template (page 104), form the wire into a foot and leg. Twist the toe and leg wires until firm.

2. Wrap each toe with strips of cloth. When each toe is wrapped, twist the fabric a couple of times around the ankle, and continue on up the leg 1¼". Trim the excess fabric. (Optional: If your fabric slips, put touches of hot glue on the wire bit by bit just ahead of where you are wrapping.)

3. Stitch as you wrap the embroidery thread around the foot and leg to secure the cloth to the wire.

4. Cut a tiny hole in the fabric at the dot on the hip/leg pieces. Poke the leg wire through the hole, and force through the fiberfill. You may need to make a pathway through the fiberfill first with a knitting needle or thick wire. Bend the wire at the top if there is excess.

5. Stitch the top of the wrapped leg to the fabric of the hip/leg piece where the leg and fabric touch.

Stitch leg to hip/leg piece.

6. Turn under the top edge of each hip/leg, and pin to the owl body where marked. With embroidery thread, whipstitch the leg to the body. The stitches will show.

Owl face and detailing

1. Pin the white felt eye patches to the owl face. Using a felting needle, poke through the felt and owl fabric, all the way through to the fiberfill. Keeping the needle perpendicular to the fabric, poke quickly and repeatedly until the felt has welded itself to the fabric underneath. If you don't have a felting needle, you could appliqué the eye patches.

2. Embroider the beak using a horizontal satin stitch.

3. Center the square top piece as shown below. Place one of the corners about halfway down between the eyes. Tack it down with a couple of stitches. Attempt to conceal your stitching by poking the needle underneath the edge of the top piece. Center the opposite point on the center of the back of the head. Pull down firmly, and stitch. Flip up the ear points, and tack down the fabric to each side of the head to stabilize.

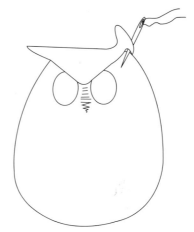

Lift sides when attaching top piece to form ears.

4. Stitch on the button eyes.

5. There are several ways to attach the feather ear tufts. The first would be to gather a little bunch of feathers in your fingers, and stitch them together securely on the cut end. When the bundle is tight, stitch it to the body fabric, deep down in the ear. If you find the stitching difficult, you could use fabric glue or hot glue to bond the feathers together, and

then attach them to the owl, deep down in the ear. The last option would be to needle felt the feathers into the ear. Don't use this method unless you feel confident with needle felting.

6. Stitch on the tail where indicated on the pattern. The jacket covers the tail area, so this is optional.

Dress the owl

1. Fold the collar piece lengthwise, and stitch the short ends. Reverse, and press. Place the raw edge of the collar, as indicated on the pattern (fold to the top), on the marked line in the neck area of the owl. Hand stitch the piece to the owl body, and then fold it down approximately in half to make the collar. Tie the ribbon into a small bow. Trim the ends, and stitch into place at the collar.

2. Using a contrasting embroidery thread, embellish the edge of the jacket by making a running stitch all the way around the cut edges. Following the line on the pattern, fold over the top edge of the jacket, and iron. Wrap the jacket around the owl body, leaving about ¼" of the shirt collar showing at the back of the neck. Overlap the jacket front, and pin to the body.

3. Turn under the raw edges of the wings, and stitch to the jacket where marked. Be sure to sew right through the jacket into the fabric of the body to keep the jacket in place.

4. Choose a nice large button, and stitch it to the center front of the jacket.

5. Spend some time bending the toes and balancing your owl. Voilà! There you have it!

Bird in a Cage

FINISHED SIZE: 8½″ × 11½″ × 8½″

It's just as well that the cage speaks volumes, as this proud bird is definitely the strong, silent type. The playful whimsy of the fancy cage is the perfect foil to the elegant embellishments on the chest and wing.

ARTIST
Jamie Christina

EMAIL
Apronstreet@yahoo.com

WEBSITES
www.phatfabric.com (shop)
www.prettyditty.com (shop)
www.jamiechristina.com

Jamie's creative journey began with her online fabric store, Phat Fabric. The abundant assortment of fabrics gave her creative energy to make clothing, aprons, and peg dolls for her Etsy.com store, Pretty Ditty. The successful reception of Jamie's clothing creations made it only natural for her to direct some of that creative energy into pattern making. Her patterns combine practical engineering with concise instructions.

MATERIALS AND CUTTING INSTRUCTIONS

Patterns are on page 104. Note: The bird seam allowance is ⅛".

Paint for painting the base and wooden beads

Paint brushes for painting and applying Mod Podge

Papier-mâché round base, approximately 4" in diameter (available at most craft stores)

4 wooden beads for the bottom of the base

Strong craft glue for gluing the wooden beads to the base

1 scrap floral fabric with at least one 4"-diameter floral motif or several smaller floral motifs (The flower will be decoupaged to the base. The example birdcage has 2 flowers decoupaged one on top of the other.):

- Cut 1 floral motif or 2 if you desire. (The flower should be approximately 4" in diameter.)

Mod Podge matte finish

4 yards 16-gauge wire:

- Vertical and circular wires: Cut 4 pieces, each 22" long.
- Scroll wire: Cut 1 piece 34" long.

¼ yard fabric for the cage wires:

- Cut 4 strips lengthwise, 1¾" × 30".

One 1¾" × 36" strip of fabric for the scrolls

Eight ½" buttons for embellishment and holding the wires together

¼ yard of felt (preferably wool felt) for the bird:

- Cut 2 bodies (1 and 1 reversed), 2 wings (1 and 1 reversed), and 1 breast.

Water-soluble fabric marker for placement markings on the bird

Embroidery floss, assorted colors, for decorating the bird and tying the bird to the cage

Polyester, cotton, or whatever stuffing you prefer for stuffing the bird

MAKE THE CAGE

Base assembly

1. Paint the base and wooden beads.

2. Once the base is dry, apply a thick layer of Mod Podge to the wrong side of the fabric flower(s), and glue it to the center of the base. Apply another layer of Mod Podge on top of the flower(s), overlapping onto the base.

3. With craft glue, glue the painted beads to the underside of the base to serve as feet for the base. Position 2 beads directly opposite each other and the remaining 2 beads opposite each other and evenly spaced between the first 2.

Vertical wire assembly

1. Fold the short ends of a 1¾″ × 30″ fabric strip in ½″ (wrong sides together), and press. Stitch the fold in place by stitching ¼″ from the folded edge.

2. Fold the fabric strip in half lengthwise (wrong sides together), and press.

3. Open the fabric strip, and fold the wrong side of the long raw edges in ¼″, and press.

4. With the raw edges folded in, refold the fabric strip in half lengthwise, and press.

5. Edgestitch along the long folded edge of the strip. The strip should now be stitched closed, with the short ends open.

6. Insert a wire into each fabric strip. The wire will be shorter than the fabric strip—this is how the gathered look is achieved.

7. Using a large safety pin, poke 4 holes into the outside edge of the base. The holes should be centered along the sides. The first 2 holes should be opposite each other, and the next 2 holes should be opposite each other and evenly spaced between the first 2 holes. If the base were a clock you would have holes at 12:00, 3:00, 6:00, and 9:00. Make sure you push the safety pin deep into the base and rotate the safety pin.

8. Gather up the fabric from the ends, revealing the wire. Poke the wire from one end through a hole in the base. Make sure at least 2" of the wire is in the base. *Hint: Hook the end of the wire before inserting it into the base. This will prevent the wire from slipping out.* Insert the opposite end of the wire into the opposite hole.

9. Repeat Steps 1–8 for the second vertical wire, inserting the ends of the wires into the 2 remaining open holes in the base.

10. Straighten the wire arches into an upright position, and pin the wires together at the top.

Circular wire assembly

1. Make the fabric strips for the circular wires the same way you did for the vertical wires (Vertical Wire Assembly, Steps 1–4). However, fold only one short end of the fabric strip, and leave the opposite end unfolded.

2. Sew the fabric strips closed. Beginning at the unfolded end, edgestitch down the length of the strip along the folded edge. Stop sewing 1" from the folded end.

3. Slide the wire through the casing, and join the opposite ends of the wire by overlapping them 1" and twisting them together.

4. Place the unfolded end of the fabric strip into the folded end. Carefully stitch the ends together by sewing along the folded edge of the fabric strip.

5. Place the circular cage wires around the cage, and pin in place. Secure them by stitching a button at each place where the vertical and circular wires meet.

Scroll wire assembly

1. To make the casing for the scrolls, follow Steps 1–4 of Vertical Wire Assembly.

2. Edgestitch along the long folded edge of the strip. Stitch one short end closed.

3. Insert the wire into the casing, and stitch the remaining short end closed.

4. Tie the wire around the top of the cage, and curl the excess wire into 2 scrolls.

MAKE THE BIRD

Embroidery stitches are on page 111.

1. Place the wrong side of the wing on the right side of the body. Embroider the wing to the body by stitching French knots along the wing.

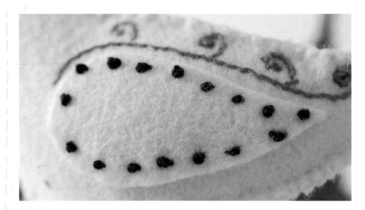

2. Continue to embroider the bird with swirls or other favorite embroidery designs. Repeat with the other wing and body. Be sure to give your bird eyes and a mouth.

3. Place one body piece on top of the other, with wrong sides together. Cut 10″ of floss, and tie a knot at one end. Place the knotted end between the body pieces. Position the floss where the bird's neck and back meet. The excess floss is outside the body. Hand stitch the body pieces together using a blanket stitch and a ⅛″ seam allowance. Begin stitching at the tip of the beak, and continue to stitch along the top of the bird, ending at the tip of the tail. *Note that the seam allowance is visible because the wrong sides are together.*

4. With wrong sides together, sew the right edge of the breast to the right side of the body. Match the black dots for placement.

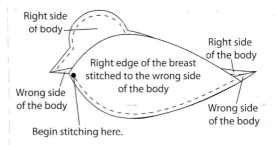

Right side of body

Right side of the body

Right edge of the breast stitched to the wrong side of the body

Wrong side of the body

Wrong side of the body

Begin stitching here.

5. Stitch the left edge of the breast to the left side of the body, leaving a 2″ opening on the left side for inserting the stuffing. Be sure to stitch closed the body pieces under the beak and tail where the breast piece does not cover.

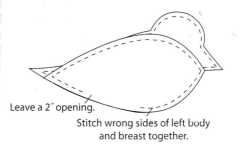

Leave a 2″ opening.

Stitch wrong sides of left body and breast together.

6. Gently insert the stuffing into the bird.

7. Hand stitch the opening closed.

8. Tie the bird to the top of the cage.

Little Round Bluebird

FINISHED SIZE: 6″ × 5″ × 5″

What this rotund little bird loses in aerodynamics, he more than makes up for with his cheerful simplicity. His shape is so irresistibly tactile, you may be just as happy to carry him everywhere anyway.

ARTIST
Laura Clempson

EMAIL
Cupcakesforclara@yahoo.com

WEBSITES
www.cupcakesforclara.com
www.cupcakesforclara.etsy.com (shop)

The award-winning label Cupcakes for Clara presents a handmade collection of beautiful toys, stationery, and home wares. A set of fictional twins, Clara and Macy—one grumpy and bossy, one quiet and sweet—set the tone for the collection. Every product is made with love, loveliness, and care.

MATERIALS AND CUTTING INSTRUCTIONS

Patterns are on page 104. Note: No seam allowances are included on the patterns.

10″ × 12″ pale blue wool felt:
- Cut 4 of Pattern A. Add ¼″ extra for the seam allowance.

Scraps of dark blue wool felt for the wings:
- Cut 4 of Pattern B.*

Scraps of brown wool felt for the feet:
- Cut 4 of Pattern C.*

Scraps of pale yellow wool felt for the beak:
- Cut 1 of Pattern D.*

Cotton thread in pale blue, dark blue, brown, and yellow

Fiberfill

Black embroidery thread for the eyes

No seam allowances are needed for B, C, and D.

CONSTRUCTION

See page 111 for embroidery stitch illustrations.

1. Pin 2 A panels together. Stitch along the seamline on one side only, using pale blue cotton thread. Repeat with the other 2 panels.

2. Pin and stitch one open edge from each set of panels together. Stitch the final open side, leaving a gap to allow for stuffing.

3. Turn right side out. Stuff the ball tightly. Carefully sew the opening closed using the ladder stitch.

4. Topstitch over the seams using dark blue cotton thread (see photo).

5. Sew the beak onto the front of the ball using yellow cotton thread. Satin stitch with black embroidery thread to create the eyes.

6. Use the blanket stitch to sew 2 wings together using pale blue cotton thread. Leave the bottom open. Carefully stuff and then sew up the opening. Repeat for the other wing and both feet. For the feet, use brown cotton thread.

7. Use the ladder stitch to securely attach each wing and foot to the ball.

Bluebird Wallets

FINISHED SIZES: 5″ × 3″

Simple and sweet, these bluebird wallets can be quickly embroidered or appliquéd. Embellished with tiny wings but having a big heart, this chubby little fellow may make you smile just by looking at him.

ARTIST
Laura Clempson

EMAIL
Cupcakesforclara@yahoo.com

WEBSITES
www.cupcakesforclara.com
www.cupcakesforclara.etsy.com (shop)

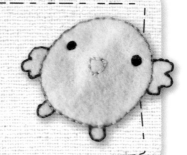

MATERIALS AND SUPPLIES

6″ × 11″ pale green wool felt for the wallet

6″ × 11″ patterned fabric for the wallet

Scrap of pale blue wool felt for the bluebird

Scrap of dark blue wool felt for the wings

Scrap of brown wool felt for the feet

Scrap of pale yellow wool felt for the beak

Cotton thread in pale blue, dark blue, brown, and yellow

Embroidery thread in blue, brown, yellow, and black

½″ button

Fray Stop

CONSTRUCTION

The bluebird pattern is on page 103.

1. Cut 1 rectangle 5″ × 9″ from pale green wool felt. Mark the positions of the button and buttonhole as shown below. Cut another rectangle 5″ × 9″ from patterned fabric. Use Fray Stop on the fabric edges, as the raw edges will be visible. *Note: No seam allowances are needed.*

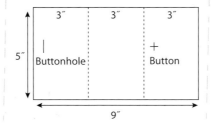

2. Use your favorite appliqué or embroidery method to create a bluebird on the front of the green wool felt. Refer to the project photo for placement.

3. Securely sew a button to the felt.

4. Pin and sew the 2 rectangles cut 5″ × 9″ together ¼″ from the edge.

5. Make a slit in the wallet where the buttonhole will go. Tightly stitch over the edges to create the buttonhole.

6. Fold up the bottom third of the wallet (the third with the button, not the bluebird), and pin, creating a pouch. Sew the side edges to secure.

Mildred the Dove with Baguettes

FINISHED DOVE SIZE: 5″ × 6″ × 3″

Mildred stops to warm her wings on the way back from the bakery as she tries to shake that nagging feeling that she has forgotten something.

ARTIST
Samantha Cotterill

EMAIL
Samcott@hotmail.com

WEBSITES
www.mummysam.etsy.com (shop)
www.sammisofties.blogspot.com (blog)

Samantha started mummysam as a means to create beautiful, one-of-a-kind fiber art inspired by her English upbringing. Each piece is lovingly made with 100% wool felt, cotton, and pure lambswool stuffing (straight from an East Coast farm!).

MATERIALS AND CUTTING INSTRUCTIONS

Patterns are on page 105.

7″ × 12″ white wool felt for the body and wings:

- Cut 1 dove body.
- Cut 1 dove left wing.
- Cut 1 dove right wing.

9″ × 5″ light yellow wool felt for the jacket:

- Cut 1 jacket.

4″ × 3″ dark yellow wool felt for the sweater:

- Cut 1 sweater.

8″ × 5″ red wool felt for the bread bag:

- Cut 2 bags.
- Cut 1 bag gusset.
- Cut 1 bag handle.

2½″ × 4″ tan wool felt for the bread loaves:

- Cut 2 baguettes.

11″ × 7″ patterned cotton for the bird body, wings, and bread loaves:

- Cut 1 dove body (reversed) for the back of the bird.
- Cut 2 baguettes for the back of the bread loaves.
- Cut 1 left wing (reversed) for the back of the left wing.
- Cut 1 right wing (reversed) for the back of the right wing.

Light blue and dark brown embroidery floss

Fabric scraps for wrapping the bird legs

Wire (16 gauge) for the bird legs:
- Cut 1 piece 9½" long for the legs.
- Cut 2 pieces 3" long for the toes.

1 small button for the jacket

Fiberfill

Hot glue

Fabric glue (or any decoupage glue)

CONSTRUCTION

See page 111 for embroidery stitch illustrations.

1. Transfer Mildred's body design to the white felt using your preferred transfer method. Using the pattern as a guide, embroider over the transferred lines using a backstitch. (Note: See project photo on page 49 as a suggestion for the color of thread to use for each particular section.)

2. Embroider the stitch lines on the sweater pattern with a backstitch using light blue embroidery floss. Attach the sweater to the front of the bird using either a sewing machine or hand stitch of your preference.

3. For each wing, embroider the design on white felt with a backstitch using dark brown embroidery floss. Place the felt wing right sides together with the wing cut from the patterned fabric of your choice. Sew ⅛" from the edge, making sure to leave the top of the wing open. Trim, and turn each piece right side out through the opening. Set aside.

4. Place Mildred's felt body right sides together with the fabric body. Sew around the outside of the bird, keeping a ⅛" distance from the edge of the design and leaving a 2" opening at the base. Trim off the extra felt and fabric, and carefully cut little notches around any curved sections to allow for a smoother shape when finished. Turn the bird right side out through the opening, and stuff the tail and head.

5. To prepare the wire legs, bend the long wire in half. Bend 1¼" at the bottom of each end to create the foot. Bend the 2 remaining wire pieces into a U shape, and hot glue 1 piece into place on top of each foot. Cut ¼"-wide strips of scrap fabric, and moisten with a quick run under the tap. Proceed to wrap the fabric around the wire until the legs and feet are completely covered. Simply brush over the entire leg with fabric glue, and let dry. Push the wired legs into the body, and finish stuffing the bird, thus securing the legs inside the body. Using any scrap wool felt available, cut out a piece of wool slightly larger than the opening left at the base of the bird. Tuck the fabric under the opening, and whipstitch into place (see

photo below). Bend Mildred's legs as necessary to create a free-standing position.

6. Using light blue embroidery floss, blanket stitch around the entire outside edge of the yellow felt jacket. Turn the collar over, and position the jacket around the bird. Pin the jacket into place once you are happy with its placement. Attach the jacket under the front collar with a stitched button on one side and a couple of hidden stitches on the other.

7. Pin the 2 wings into their desired positions. (Have fun with this. By simply changing the direction and position of the wings, you can really personalize your bird.) Attach the top of each wing to the bird's body with a whipstitch.

8. Attach the bag sides to either side of the gusset using a blanket stitch in yellow embroidery floss. Attach the strap on either side of the bag using a simple cross-stitch.

9. Embroider a design on the tan felt loaves of bread using dark brown floss. Place the felt bread loaf and the fabric bread loaf right sides together. Sew ⅛" from the edge, making sure to leave a 1" opening along one edge. Trim off any extra fabric, and turn the bread piece right side out through the opening. Stuff the loaf of bread, and sew shut with a whipstitch in the thread color of your choice. Repeat this process for the second loaf of bread.

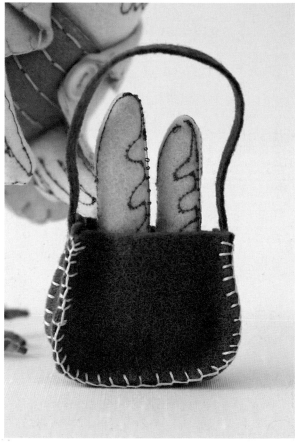

Birds on a Wire
Quilt

FINISHED QUILT SIZE: 30″ × 18″

Friends are never far away in this fanciful quilted wallhanging. Use your favorite appliqué method, raid your stash for the colorful fabrics, and create a project that will have everyone talking.

ARTIST
Alicia Diane Durand

WEBSITE
www.thislittlefish.etsy.com (shop)

Alicia Diane Durand of This Little Fish combines a strong sense of color and childlike drawings to create dynamic, playful, engaging fiber art. She loves to share her stories with markers and fabric. Her quilts are fun to make and a joy to give or a treasure to keep.

MATERIALS AND CUTTING INSTRUCTIONS

For the appliqué, create templates from the patterns on pages 105–106. Trace the templates onto fusible web, follow the product directions to iron, and trim.

⅝ yard light blue print fabric:

- Cut 1 rectangle 32″ × 20″ for the background.

¼ yard green fabrics:

- Cut 2 strips 3½″ × 32″ for the contrasting hills. Cut a wavy line down the middle to create the hills.

Cut wavy line.

Assorted scraps of brown fabrics:

- Cut 2 rectangles ¾″ × 15″ for the telephone poles.
- Cut 2 rectangles ½″ × 4″ for the telephone pole tops.
- Cut 3 strips ½″ × 4″ for the tree trunks.

Assorted scraps of solid fabrics:

- Cut 6 of Pattern A for the bird bodies.
- Cut 6 of Pattern B for the bird wings.
- Cut 6 of Pattern C for the bird beaks.
- Cut 2 of Pattern D for the treetops.
- Cut 3 of Pattern E for the treetops.
- Cut 3 of Pattern F for the treetops.
- Cut 2 of Pattern G for the treetops.
- Cut 1 of Pattern H for the treetops.

⅛ yard white fabric:

- Cut 1 small cloud from pattern I. Enlarge pattern to create medium and large clouds.

¼ yard binding fabric:

- Cut 3 strips 2½″ × 40″ for double-fold binding.

¾ yard backing and sleeve fabric:

- Cut 36″ × 24″ for the backing.
- Cut 6″ × 30″ for sleeve (optional).

36″ × 24″ batting

6 buttons ¼″ in diameter for birds' eyes

1 yard paper-backed iron-on fusible web (17″ wide)

Coordinating thread for satin stitching

Fabric chalk

QUILT ASSEMBLY

1. Layer the backing fabric (right side down), batting, and light blue print fabric (right side up).

2. Pin together.

3. Quilt a long wavy stitch across the middle with coordinating thread. Quilt rows above and below, spaced 1″ apart. Continue until the entire quilt is quilted.

APPLIQUÉ

1. Arrange the hills, telephone poles, and tree trunks, and iron down. Satin stitch the edges with coordinating thread. Add 2 satin stitch lines, ¼″ thick, at the top of the telephone pole for the wire to cross. Satin stitch the diagonal supports for the telephone pole tops.

Quilt layout

2. Draw the 2 telephone pole wires with fabric chalk, and stitch with black thread.

3. Arrange the bird bodies, wings, beaks, treetops, and clouds, and then iron the pieces down. Satin stitch the edges with coordinating thread.

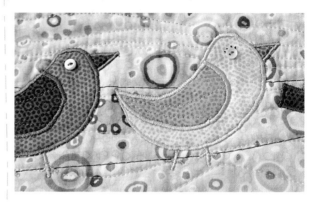

QUILTING AND FINISHING

1. Quilt the hills and bird wings with coordinating thread.

2. Sew 6 buttons (¼″ diameter) for the bird eyes. Hand sew with embroidery thread 4 lashes per bird.

3. Sew the bird feet with a narrow satin stitch.

Bird feet

4. Trim the quilt to approximately 30″ × 18″.

5. Bind the quilt. Add a hanging sleeve, if desired.

Embroidered Doorknob Ornament

FINISHED SIZE: 3½" × 4" × ¼"

This calm and restful bird, perched among the cherry blossoms, is sure to bring a touch of serene springtime to your stitchery.

ARTIST
Lisa Fell

EMAIL
Lisa@lazymay.com

WEBSITE
www.lazymay.com

isa Fell loves embroidery and all things crafty. She designs all the patterns she sells. Lazy May is the home of cute, quirky, and original iron-on embroidery patterns. Quick and easy to use, Lazy May iron-on patterns lead to great results—fast.

MATERIALS AND SUPPLIES

2 squares 8″ × 8″ of natural cotton muslin

1 square 8″ × 8″ of ⅛″ flat batting

18″ cream-colored satin ribbon (approximately ½″ width)

Embroidery floss in light brown, dark brown, yellow, pink, white, and dark gray

Pink coloring pencil

Embroidery hoop

CONSTRUCTION

The pattern is on page 109. Refer to page 111 for embroidery stitch diagrams.

1. Use a pencil to trace the pattern onto the fabric; do not trace the outer oval yet.

2. Color the flower petals lightly with the pink coloring pencil.

3. Begin to embroider the design onto the fabric. Use a small split stitch along the lines of the bird and a small backstitch for the branches, leaves, and blossoms.

4. Once the embroidery is finished, lay the fabric right side down over the pattern again, and trace the oval with a pencil so it is on the back of the fabric.

5. To assemble the hanger, fold the ribbon in half and place on the fabric as shown, and pin. Place the backing (right side facing the right side of the embroidery) and batting on top, and pin.

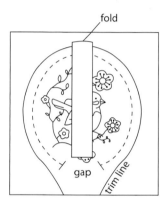

6. Turn the stack over, and sew along the penciled oval. Make sure to go through all the layers of fabric, batting, and ribbon. Use a small, tight backstitch, and follow the lines of the oval to secure the fabric layers together. Leave a gap of about 1½″ in your stitching.

7. Trim around the oval. Now turn the embroidery inside out; the easiest way to do this is to pull on the ribbon.

8. Once the hanger is right side out, tuck the excess fabric back into the gap, and shape to complete the oval. Secure in place with small, neat stitches. Tie your thread, and trim the ends.

Mid-Century Scrap Quilt

FINISHED QUILT SIZE: APPROXIMATELY 40" × 50"

This quilt is a fresh interpretation of the classic family tree. Add embroidered names for a personal touch, or let the oversized appliqué speak for itself.

ARTIST

Nancy DeWeir Geaney

WEBSITE

www.darkhorsefarmdesigns.com

Nancy learned her sewing technique from her seventh-grade home ec teacher, as well as at home, from her three sisters, mom, and grandmother. She went on to become a fashion model, and *Vogue Patterns* magazine even did a feature story, "Nancy Sews." The needles and pins were put away for a time when her daughter and son were small, but emerged again with a vengeance about ten years ago. With the inspiration and encouragement of Sis Boom designer Jennifer Paganelli, Nancy started designing and sewing quilts of her own.

MATERIALS AND CUTTING INSTRUCTIONS

44″ × 60″ fabric for the backing

44″ × 60″ muslin (or other fabric) for the quilt top background

¼ yard fabric for the tree trunk:

- Cut (or piece together) a trunk that is 31″ tall and 5½″ wide at the base, narrowing to ¾″ wide at the top (see diagram on page 63).

½ yard fabric for the binding

44″ × 60″ piece of batting

8 sheets Lite Steam-A-Seam 2 or similar double-sided iron-on fusible web

10–12 fabric scraps with various patterns and in different sizes to fit the templates (A combination of stripes, dots, patterns, and solids works well for the birds, nests, leaves, eggs, small trees, and flowers.)

CONSTRUCTION

Patterns are on page 107.

1. Cut pieces of fusible web to fit the fabric scraps. Cut just smaller than the fabric to protect the iron. Follow the instructions on the package. Leave enough room for drawing the template shapes.

2. Draw the template shapes on the paper side of the fusible web, and fuse to the wrong side of the fabric. Cut out the desired shapes.

3. Add fusible web to the back of trunk fabric. Cut (or piece together) a trunk that is 31″ tall and 5½″ wide at the base, narrowing to ¾″ wide at the top. Add branches such as shown in the illustration on page 63. Start by placing the tree trunk in the center of the quilt, being sure to leave room at the top for the nest (approximately 14″ from the top). Then sew with the buttonhole

stitch. I used a larger stitch width and longer stitch setting for the trees, birds, and nests, and a smaller, tighter setting for the eggs and leaves. Satin stitch would also work nicely.

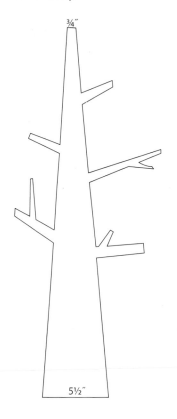

4. Using the project photo as a guide, add nests, birds, and eggs, one nest at a time. Feel free to create your own nests, birds, and eggs in various sizes. Add small trees. Press, and sew.

5. Add leaves, press, and sew.

6. Layer the quilt back, batting, and top. Quilt as desired.

7. Trim and bind.

Pikku the Penguin

FINISHED SIZE: 5″ × 6″ × 4″

Pikku the Penguin brings Parisian chic to the South Pole. With his jaunty hat and sensible scarf, he is ready for any winter day of play.

ARTIST
Melanie Hurlston

EMAIL
mellyandme@optusnet.com.au

WEBSITE
www.mellyandme.typepad.com (blog)

Melanie is an Australian pattern designer working under the pattern label "Melly & me." She designs a range of contemporary sewing patterns that include bright and quirky toys and wearable purses, as well as fun, modern quilts. She aims to design items that are original, fun, and achievable in a day, as well as being completely usable in everyday life.

MATERIALS AND CUTTING INSTRUCTIONS

Patterns are on page 108.

¼ yard black print fabric for the main body and base:

- Cut 4 heads (2 and 2 reversed).
- Cut 4 bodies.
- Cut 1 outer base.

10″ × 10″ white print fabric for the tummy, eye patch, wings, and feet

5″ × 5″ fusible web for the tummy and eye patch

5″ × 5″ iron-on Pellon nonwoven fusible interfacing for the feet and wings

4″ × 4″ heavy, strong cardboard for the inner base:

- Cut 1 base using the inner line.

Small scraps of blue, orange, and black wool felt for the eyes and beak

- Cut 2 blue outer eyes.
- Cut 2 black inner eyes.
- Cut 2 orange beaks.

4″ × 14″ green wool felt for the scarf and beret:

- Cut a strip ½″ × 14″ for the scarf.

1 small black curved button for the beret

6-strand embroidery floss in black, green, blue, and white

Good-quality polyester toy fiberfill

2. Place 2 head pieces right sides together, so that the edges and darts meet. Sew together along the center seam. Repeat with the remaining head pieces.

3. Place 2 body pieces right sides together, and sew together along the center seam. Repeat with the remaining body pieces.

4. Affix fusible web to a 4" × 6" piece of white print fabric. Trace the tummy and eye patch templates, and cut out on the lines. Center the tummy on the front of the body, and the eye patch on the front of the face. Iron, and machine appliqué into place.

5. Take the remaining white print fabric, and iron Pellon to half of this. Fold in half, right sides together, and trace the foot and wing templates twice. Sew together along the traced lines, leaving gaps open as indicated. Trim ¼" outside the sewn line. Turn right side out, and press.

6. Place the body back and head back right sides together, so that the neck edges meet. Sew together along the neck. Repeat for Pikku's front.

7. Place the front and back pieces right sides together. Sew the body together, leaving the bottom edge open for the base.

8. Stuff the feet lightly with fiberfill. Tack 1 foot over the left side of the tummy patch, right sides together. The raw edge of the foot should meet the bottom edge of the body. Repeat for the right foot.

CONSTRUCTION

Patterns are on page 108.

All seam allowances are ¼".

1. Take 1 head piece, and sew the dart in place. Repeat with the remaining 3 head pieces.

9. With the body inside out, ease the base into position, right sides together, along the bottom body edge. Tack and sew the base into position, from one marked star to the other. Turn right side out. Insert cardboard into the gap against the base.

10. Stuff firmly with fiber fill, ensuring that the cardboard remains in place. Ladder stitch the gap closed, working around the cardboard base piece.

11. Stuff the wings lightly with fiber fill. Ladder stitch the opening closed, and then stitch the wings into position on the body sides.

12. Trace and cut out 2 beak pieces from orange felt. Sew together along the V edge only, and turn. Ladder stitch the bottom edge into position. Lightly stuff the beak, and then ladder stitch the top edge into place.

13. Iron fusible web to the blue and black felt scraps. Trace the eye template twice onto blue felt, and the pupil twice onto black felt. Cut out the shapes, peel away the paper, and press the eyes into position. Using 2 strands of matching floss, blanket stitch the eyes in place. Mark the eyebrows, and backstitch these using 3 stands of black floss. Create a dot in each pupil with a white French knot. Refer to page 111 for embroidery stitches.

14. Tie the ½" × 14" green felt strip on Pikku like a scarf. Trim and snip the ends to create a fringe.

15. Sew the 2 green beret pieces together close to the line. Snip the bottom circle ONLY as marked, and use this gap to turn. Stuff lightly, and ladder stitch onto Pikku's head. Attach a curved button to the top of the beret, taking the stitch into the head.

16. Using 6 strands of floss, create a tuft of hair. Pass the needle through the top center seam of the head, and tie the ends in a square knot. Trim the ends to approximately ½" in length. Repeat as desired.

Garden of Birds Embroidery

FINISHED EMBROIDERY SIZE: 10" × 8" **FINISHED PILLOW SIZE:** 15" × 13" × 2½"

A trio of homes entices these birds to each pick a favorite. Classic redwork provides a crisp cottage accent to any room.

ARTIST
Robin Kingsley

EMAIL
Robin@birdbraindesigns.net

WEBSITE
www.BirdBrainDesigns.net

Robin Kingsley has been indulging in needlework of some kind or another it seems forever! It began with very primitive and simple embroidery when pregnant with her son over 40 years ago. Now needlework in the form of Bird Brain Designs has become a terrific livelihood for her and her sister, Tina. Embroidery continues to be her favorite needlework, especially redwork—the most relaxing type of embroidery!

MATERIALS AND CUTTING INSTRUCTIONS

See page 110 for pattern.

14″ × 12″ piece of muslin

½ yard red-and-white print fabric:

- Cut 2 strips 3″ × 10½″ for the top and bottom borders.
- Cut 2 strips 3″ × 13½″ for the side borders.
- Cut 1 piece 15½″ × 13½″ for the pillow back.

15½″ × 13½″ piece of thin batting

1 ball #498 Turkey red #8 perle cotton

#4 crewel needle

1 permanent red 01 Pigma marker for transferring the design

1 bag of polyester fiberfill

EMBROIDERY

Refer to page 111 for embroidery stitch diagrams.

1. To transfer the design, tape the pattern on a lightbox or a bright window. Tape the muslin over the pattern. With a permanent-ink Pigma marker, draw your design directly onto the muslin.

Note: You do not need to transfer broken lines for running stitch or loops for lazy daisy stitches; just stitch "by eye" from the pattern.

2. Use #8 perle cotton or 3 strands of embroidery floss for the embroidery. Lines are backstitch, dots are French knots, broken lines are running stitch, and loops are lazy daisy stitch. Use satin stitch for the eggs in the nest and for the flower centers.

FINISH THE EMBROIDERY

1. If needed, wash the finished embroidery in sudsy water with a large dollop of white vinegar to set the Turkey red color. Rinse well and dry on a towel.

2. Place the embroidery on a soft towel, and iron from the wrong side. Use a little spray starch to help while you iron.

MAKE THE PILLOW TOP

All seam allowances are ¼".

1. Square up and cut the finished embroidery to 10½" × 8½" (¼" seam allowance included).

2. Stitch 3" × 10½" strips to the top and bottom of the embroidery. Press the seams to the outside.

3. Stitch a 3" × 13½" strip to each side of the embroidery. Press the seams to the outside.

4. Baste a piece of thin batting to the wrong side of the pillow top.

5. With #8 perle cotton, embroider a running-stitch line around the embroidery just inside the red-and-white strips. Add a French knot in each corner.

FINISH THE PILLOW

1. Align the pillow top and back with right sides together, and stitch around the pillow, leaving a 6" opening on one side to turn.

2. Turn right side out, and press the seam edges.

3. Make a flange edge around the pillow by machine stitching ¾" in from the outside edge. Begin and end at the opening.

4. Stuff the pillow with fiberfill, and hand stitch the opening closed.

5. Complete the flange edge on your machine.

Bird's Nest Journal

FINISHED SIZE: 8″ × 11″ × ¾″

If this book were to be judged by its cover, inspiration would surely be inside. Collaged using burlap, lace, and fabric, this textured journal makes a thoughtful gift.

ARTIST
Kimberly Laws

EMAIL
Kimlaws@verizon.net

WEBSITES
www.artjoystuff.etsy.com/ (shop)
http://artjoystuff.typepad.com/art-joy-stuff/ (blog)

Kimberly Laws is a mixed-media collage and assemblage artist. She generally works with paper but is never far from her sewing machine, as most of her pieces feature paper, fabric, vintage lace, and trim stitched together. "I am an avid 'junker,' and many of my vintage treasures find their way into my work."

MATERIALS AND SUPPLIES

8" × 8" square of fabric for the bird

7 squares 3" × 3" of various fabrics for the egg, wing, letters, and head feathers

5" × 5" square of fabric for the nest

9" × 12" fabric for the back cover

5" × 5" square of fusible web

8" × 12" dark brown craft felt for appliqué background layer

10" × 7" vintage lace for the front cover

16" × 11" burlap for the journal cover

2 sheets 12" × 12" scrapbook paper for the inside covers

Button for the bird's eye

Black-and-white composition book

Dark brown thread

Craft glue

Inside front cover

CUTTING AND ASSEMBLY

Patterns are on page 108.

1. Make templates from the patterns. Arrange the templates for bird, wing, head feathers, egg, and the letters on the right side of the fabrics. Pin, and cut.

2. Following the manufacturer's directions, iron fusible web to the back side of the nest fabric. Allow the piece to cool, and remove the backing. Using a rotary cutter or scissors, cut into ¼" strips.

3. Place brown craft felt on a flat work surface. Arrange the nest strips with the fusible side facing the felt. Be sure to overlap, change the angles, and shorten some of the strips until the arrangement is pleasing. Cover the work with a piece of parchment paper before ironing; be very careful not to burn the felt.

4. Arrange and pin the other cut pieces onto the felt. Place the egg in the nest, the bird on the egg, and the wing on the bird, and tuck the head feathers under the bird's head. The letters may be pinned randomly.

5. Outline each piece using a straight stitch. Make 2 passes in a very loose style. This may be done free-motion or traditionally.

6. Cut the nest, egg, and bird out as one piece and the letters individually, leaving a scant edge of the brown felt as an outline.

7. Wrap the composition book in burlap, and attach the burlap using craft glue. Fray the edges of the burlap by pulling one thread a time, removing 4–5 threads from each side. Center and glue vintage lace to the front cover.

8. Sew on a button for the bird's eye. Arrange and glue the bird and nest piece and letters to the lace.

FINISHING

1. Snip and tear the edges of the 9" × 12" piece of fabric for the back cover. Be sure that the final size fits nicely on the book. Attach the fabric over the burlap on the outside back cover with glue.

Back of journal

2. Cut 2 pieces of coordinating scrapbook paper or other decorative paper to fit the inside front and back covers. Apply a thin, even layer of craft glue to the cover, attach the paper, and smooth.

Bird in a Rag Nest

FINISHED SIZE OF NEST: 6″ × 6″ × 3″   **FINISHED SIZE OF BIRD:** 2½″ × 3″ × 1″

Look who has just hatched! This delicate little chick is just finding his feet as he leaves his knitted nest, perhaps asking, "Are you my mother?"

ARTIST
Margaret Oomen

EMAIL
Margaretoomen@mac.com

WEBSITES
www.resurrectionfern.typepad.com
www.knitalette.etsy.com

Margaret Oomen, a rural physician and textile artist, draws her inspiration from her treasure-hunting family, her scientific and medical background, and her great love of the natural world. Her work has been featured in *Country Living* magazine, *Design*Sponge*, *Apartment Therapy*, *Elle Décor SA*, Glam.com, the *ReadyMade* blog, *Whip Up*, the *Craftzine.com* blog, *Softies Central*, and *Plush You*.

MATERIALS AND CUTTING INSTRUCTIONS

Patterns are on page 109.

1 yard vintage bed sheet or other cotton fabric for the knitted nest

4 double-pointed knitting needles, size 15 (10mm)

Yarn needle

Tracing paper

12″ × 12″ square of yellow felt for the bird body:

- Cut 2 faces (1 and 1 reversed).
- Cut 1 bird body.
- Cut 1 tail.
- Cut 2 (1 and 1 reversed) wings.
- Cut 1 top of head.

Scrap of white felt for the cheeks:

- Cut 2 cheeks.

Scrap of orange felt for the beak:

- Cut 1 beak.

Remnant of printed fabric:

- Cut 2 (1 and 1 reversed) wings.
- Cut 1 tail (reversed).

Scrap of fabric to wrap bird legs.

- Cut 1 strip ¼″ × 20″.

Fiberfill or suitable stuffing material

Embroidery floss in black, white, and a color that matches the body

12″ of 20-gauge wire

- Cut into 3 pieces of wire each approximately 3″ long.

MAKE THE KNITTED RAG NEST

1. Tear the 1-yard piece of fabric into strips ½" wide. Don't cut—tear. It really makes a difference in the nest's appearance. When you need to join the strips, just tie a knot, leaving some ends. These will add character to the finished product. Roll up the torn fabric into a ball.

2. Cast on 36 stitches, divided evenly on 3 needles.

3. Join the round and knit for 6 rounds.

4. Next start the decreases to shape the nest. Knit (k) 4 stitches and then knit 2 together (k2tog), and repeat this until you have completed a round. You should have 28 stitches remaining. Knit 1 round.

5. Next round: k3 stitches and then k2tog, and repeat this until you have completed the round. You will have 21 stitches remaining. Knit 1 round.

6. Next round: k2 stitches and k2tog, and repeat this until the end of the round. Knit 1 round. K1 and then k2tog, and repeat until the end of the round. Knit 1 round. You should have a total of 12 stitches remaining.

7. Cut the rag strip about 12" long, and thread it into a yarn needle. Thread it through each stitch, and pull to gather up the last 12 stitches tightly. Fasten the end securely. Weave in ends.

MAKE THE BIRD

The pieces are all hand sewn using a blanket stitch with matching embroidery floss. Refer to page 111 for embroidery stitch illustrations.

1. Stitch the cheek pieces to the face. Add the eye detail using a French knot or a small black seed bead.

2. Starting with the head, sew both sides of the top head piece to the face pieces.

3. Sew the bottom of the face pieces together, but remember to stuff the head before sewing it closed.

4. Fold the beak, and sew it on the fold line to the face, using the photograph (page 78) as a guide.

5. Fold the body in half, and sew it together, stuffing it before it is sewn closed.

6. Layering the printed fabric on top of the felt with wrong sides together, baste the wings and tail pieces together with a simple running stitch.

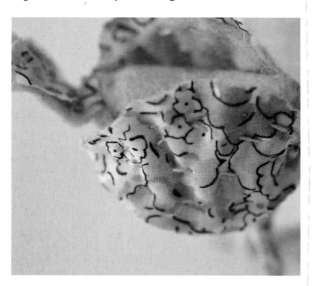

7. Sew the tail and wings to the body, keeping wings loose on top.

8. Sew the head onto the body.

9. Wrap each of the cut wire pieces individually with ¼" fabric strips, and then wrap them all together using the following diagram and photo as guides

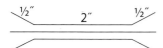

Wrap wires tying the middle 2" of 3 wires together and leaving outside ends free for toes.

10. Bend the wrapped wire in half, and carefully poke it through the middle bottom of the body where you have sewn. Shape the wire to suit you and to give the bird balance.

Little Birds Quilt

FINISHED QUILT SIZE: 18½" × 16"

It's difficult to pick a favorite from among this fanciful flock. Simple piecing, careful fabric selection, and inspired machine stitching work together to create an accent quilt suitable for any nook in the house.

ARTIST
Anita Peluso

EMAIL
bloominworkshop@gmail.com

WEBSITE
www.bloominworkshop.com

Anita designs quilt patterns sold primarily through a local quilt shop and distributed by a local fabric manufacturer. Between designing and making quilts, she teaches beginning quilting techniques and blogs about her quilting adventures.

MATERIALS AND CUTTING INSTRUCTIONS

⅓ yard total various blue print fabrics for the horizontal pieced strips

⅛ yard total various red print fabrics for the horizontal pieced strips

- From the red and blue print fabrics: Cut approximately 40 rectangles ranging from 1½″ to 2½″ in width and 3″ in height.

Assorted scraps of red, blue, and green fabrics for the appliquéd birds

¼ yard muslin for the appliqué background:

- Cut 2 strips 4½″ × 18½″.

¼ yard fabric for the binding:

- Cut 2 strips 2½″ × 40″ for double-fold binding.

⅝ yard fabric for the backing:

- Cut a 22″ × 20″ rectangle.

22″ × 20″ batting

¼ yard paper-backed fusible web (17″ wide)

Brown thread for sketchy stitching around the appliquéd birds

QUILT ASSEMBLY

Patterns are on page 110.

Note: All seam allowances are ¼".

1. Referring to the project photo on page 81, arrange and sew the blue and red rectangles into 3 horizontal strips measuring approximately 19" in width. Trim each strip to 3" × 18½".

2. Arrange the 3 horizontal pieced strips alternately with the muslin strips to create the quilt top. The quilt should now measure 16" × 18½".

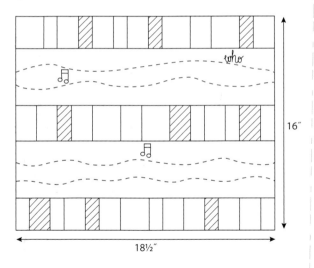

BIRD APPLIQUÉ

1. Trace the bird body shapes and owl body parts to the paper-backed fusible web.

2. Cut apart the shapes, but do not trim, so that each can be adhered to a piece of scrap fabric.

3. Following the fusible web manufacturer's instructions, adhere each bird body shape to a scrap of fabric.

4. Carefully trim around each body shape, and remove the paper backing.

5. Lightly position the bird shapes on the 2 muslin strips of the quilt. Arrange the shapes until you are happy with their placement.

6. Iron the shapes in place to permanently adhere them to the quilt top.

QUILTING AND FINISHING

1. Layer and baste the quilt.

2. Machine quilt the horizontal pieced strips by stitching in the ditch.

3. Sketchy stitch around the bird and owl appliqués (see sketchy stitching tips below).

4. Machine quilt 2 wavy horizontal lines across the bird panels, stopping and starting or stitching around the bird bodies. Add musical note details if desired.

5. Bind the quilt.

SKETCHY STITCHING

1. Prepare the sewing machine for free-motion quilting, dropping the feed dogs and using a darning or stippling foot. Using brown contrasting thread, sew 2 or 3 stitches in place to secure the thread. Stitch around the bird shape once.

2. Stitch around the shape again, randomly weaving from left to right over the first stitching line, sometimes stitching on the bird fabric and other times off the bird fabric. Don't worry about stitching perfectly around the shape. Part of the charm of this technique is the random uneven sewing on and off the shape. Stitch around the shape a total of 3 or 4 times. On the final round, add the beak, the plumes, and the feet details.

3. Cut the thread, and stitch the eye and the wing in the same manner as the body. Repeat for remaining birds.

Owl Wallhanging

FINISHED SIZE: 10″ × 10″ × ½″

This wide-awake owl doesn't miss a thing from his perch on a button-bedecked branch. Render him in super-simple stitchery and bright fabrics for a quick and easy gift.

ARTIST

Sharon Smith

WEBSITES

www.lovesnoam.etsy.com (shop)

www.smithfamilysmith.blogspot.com (blog)

Sharon is based in Birmingham, Alabama. Her online store features fiber arts, embroidered wallhangings, and jewelry. Sharon finds inspiration in God, nature, music, animals, fashion, and fabrics. In addition to crafting, Sharon works as a mental health therapist and enjoys spending time with her husband, cats, and Great Dane.

MATERIALS AND CUTTING INSTRUCTIONS

Patterns are on page 109.

10″ wooden embroidery hoop

12″ × 12″ linen or burlap for the background

1 fat quarter (18″ × 22″) fabric for the owl body appliqué and backing:

- Cut 1 owl body for appliqué.
- Cut a 12″ × 12″ square for the backing.

4″ × 4″ fabric for the owl belly appliqué:

- Cut 1 owl belly for appliqué.

4″ × 4″ felt for the eye background in a color to match the fabric:

- Cut 2 eye circles.

2 wooden buttons 1⅛″ in diameter for the eye centers

5 buttons of various colors that match the fabric for the tree's flowers

5 skeins of embroidery floss (3 colors of your choice and 1 green and 1 brown)

½ yard ribbon for hanger

CONSTRUCTION

Note: For embroidery, use all 6 strands of embroidery floss. See page 111 for embroidery stitches.

1. Place the linen or burlap tightly in the embroidery hoop.

2. Using the project photo as a reference, attach the owl body appliqué to the linen or burlap with floss using a running stitch.

3. Center the owl belly appliqué on top of the body appliqué, and attach with floss using a running stitch.

4. Arrange the felt circles for the eye background, and attach with a running stitch.

5. Sew on the 1⅛" wooden buttons for eyes.

6. Embroider the feet of the owl in brown embroidery floss using a split stitch.

7. Draw the tree branch, and embroider it in green embroidery floss using a split stitch.

8. Sew on buttons for the flowers.

9. Place the backing fabric on the back of the hoop, and tuck in the edges. Tack in place using a running stitch. Fold the edges of the linen or burlap under the backing as you stitch.

10. Thread ribbon through the clamp of the embroidery hoop, and tie it in a bow for the hanger.

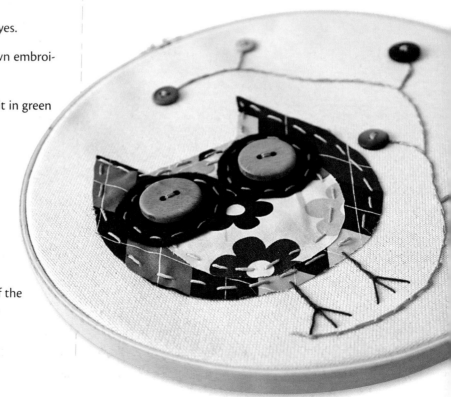

FINISHED SIZE: 2″ × 8″ × 1¼″

Budgie

Lifelike and handsome, this budgerigar has all the charm of the real deal without the messy cleanup! This project provides a wonderful opportunity to show off the intricate details that can be achieved through simple stitches. Make one budgie or create a colorful collection.

ARTIST
Jantze Tullett

EMAIL
jantze@ntlworld.com

WEBSITES
jantzetullett.co.uk
http://jantze.wordpress.com/ (blog)
jantzetullett.etsy.com (shop)

Jantze Tullett is an artist living and working in England. She trained at Edinburgh College of Art and loves sewing, drawing, and printmaking. Jantze is inspired by childhood memories, wildlife, and nature—and by her daily life with a young family. Her work is available through Etsy.com.

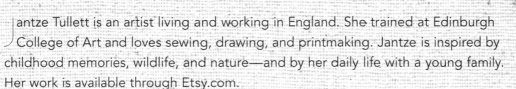

MATERIALS AND CUTTING INSTRUCTIONS

Patterns are on page 108.

8" × 9" purple 100% wool felt:

- Cut 2 of budgie body (1 and 1 reversed).
- Cut 1 gusset.

3" × 6" white 100% wool felt:

- Cut 2 heads (1 and 1 reversed).

Thick perle cotton thread #8 in black, purple, and white

Fine perle cotton thread #12 in black, purple, and white

Small amount of purple and blue (brown for the female) sewing thread for details

Metallic gold thread for the beak

2 gray or silver sequins for the eyes

Natural or synthetic fiberfill (approximately 1 oz.)

CONSTRUCTION

Note: There are no seam allowances. See page 111 for embroidery stitch illustrations.

Bird body

1. Place head onto body as shown below. Pin the pieces together. Repeat with the other head and body

pieces, ensuring that the 2 sides reflect each other as shown. Right sides of all pieces should face up.

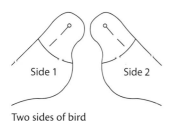

Two sides of bird

2 Start with side 1. Use fine white perle cotton thread (#12). Sew along the lower edge of head using long and short stitches. Sew 2 rows from the back of the neck and around the top of the head using long and short stitches. Repeat on side 2.

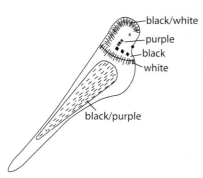

Surface stitching and placement of wings and eyes

3. Using fine black perle cotton thread (#12), sew 2 rows from the back of the neck and around the top of the head using long and short stitches. Stitch 3 spots in satin stitch. Repeat on side 2.

4. Using fine purple perle cotton thread (#12), sew a stripe along the cheek in satin stitch. Repeat on side 2.

5. Use thick perle cotton (#8) in black, purple, and white to fill in the wing area with long stitches. Combine black and purple stitches to create a feather effect. Use white to stitch a flash at the tip of each wing, as shown in the photo below.

Bird assembly

1. Place the 2 sides together, raw edges matching and wrong sides together. Pin. Using fine white perle cotton thread, stitch around the bird at the sections shown on the diagram on page 90, using a small, neat blanket stitch. Finish securely.

2 Open up the front of the bird, and fit the gusset in, matching the edges. Pin. Sew around the edge using a blanket stitch.

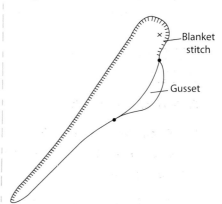

3. Fill the bird through the tail opening until it is plump and firm.

4. Sew the remaining tail section closed with a blanket stitch.

5. Using fine black perle cotton thread, sew a sequin, secured with a French knot, on either side of the head for eyes.

6. Sew the beak using gray or gold thread. Bind over the seam until the beak forms. Sew a blue stripe at the top of the beak for a male budgie, or brown for a female.

Wreath with a Bird

DIAMETER OF FINISHED WREATH: APPROXIMATELY 10½"

This deceptively easy and instantly classic wreath is the perfect project to showcase all those treasured scraps of fabric that simply can't be thrown away. Bring high-end design to any occasion.

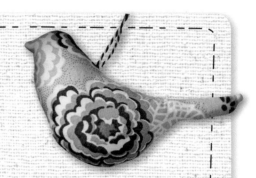

ARTIST
Noor van Krimpen

EMAIL:
Noor@chello.nl

WEBSITES
www.hollandfabrichouse.com
www.hollandfabrichouse.etsy.com

Holland Fabric House is a Dutch company founded in 2008 by Noor van Krimpen. It is a bright and cheerful place in cyberspace that offers colorful and contemporary fabrics and matching notions. The handmade collection for home, kids, and women consists of original accessories designed to bring joy and inspiration.

MATERIALS AND CUTTING INSTRUCTIONS

Metal ring with a diameter of 8″ (available from craft shops)

10 pieces of cotton fabric 4½″ × 13″ for the strips:

- Cut a total of 260 fabric strips, each measuring approximately ½″ in width and 4½″ in length. The number of strips you cut from each fabric depends on how many different types of fabric you want to include in your wreath. In this example, I used 10 different fabrics, so I cut 26 strips per fabric.

2 pieces of fabric 4″ × 6½″ for the bird

58½″ grosgrain ribbon (⅝″ width) in a matching color to cut into strips:

- Cut the ribbon into 13 pieces, each 4½″ long.

27½″ grosgrain ribbon (⅝″ wide) to hang the wreath

19½″ gingham ribbon (1″ wide) for the bow at the bottom

15½″ length of baker's twine or thin ribbon to hang the bird

Polyfill to stuff the bird

CONSTRUCTION

1. Arrange the fabric and ribbon strips. Try to create an attractive sequence of colors and prints, and follow this sequence when you tie the strips to the wreath.

Fasten the strips to the metal ring by tying a knot around the ring in the center of each strip. Start with the first strip in your sequence, and follow the sequence all the way through. Continue this process all the way around the metal ring.

Tie in the grosgrain ribbon strips every other sequence (so in sequences 1, 3, 5, etc.) to create some extra texture. After every 4 or 5 sequences, push the strips tightly together with your hands so that there is no space between them. The trick to making this wreath look stunning is making it really full!

2. When the wreath is full, create a little bit of space at the bottom of the ring by pulling a few strips apart, and tie the gingham ribbon around the ring with a knot. Finish by tying a large bow.

3. On the opposite end of the wreath, also create some space. Fold the 27½" length of grosgrain ribbon in half, and pin it in place around the ring. Hand sew the ribbon in place with a few stitches.

4. To create the bird that will hang in the center, pin 2 pieces of fabric 4" × 6½" with right sides together. On the wrong side of one piece of fabric, pin the pattern (see page 106) in place, and trace around it with a fabric marker or chalk. Do not forget to mark the opening to turn the bird right side out after sewing (marked "leave open" on pattern). Fold the baker's twine or thin ribbon in half, and pin it in place between the 2 layers of fabric in the crook of the bird's neck, with the 2 long ends inside the bird. Sew all around the traced edge, by machine or by hand. Next, cut out the bird, leaving a ¼" seam allowance all around. Turn inside out (use a pointed object to push the tail and beak out), stuff with polyfill, and carefully but firmly press the stuffing into place. Hand sew the remaining opening closed. Tie the bird next to the grosgrain ribbon at the top of the wreath, and make sure it dangles in the center.

Hang your wreath in a nice spot, step back, and *admire*.

Bird on a Branch Makeup Bag

FINISHED SIZE: 9″ × 4½″ × 2″

Take the basic to the beautiful with this stylish makeup bag. The zakka simplicity and attention to detail cleverly belie its practicality.

ARTIST
Monika Wintermantel

EMAIL
Monaw68@web.de

WEBSITES
www.de.dawanda.com/shop/monaw (German)
www.monaw.etsy.com (shop)
www.monaw.blogspot.com/ (blog)

Monika Wintermantel has loved crafting for as long as she can remember, so creating bags and accessories using all kind of fabrics (old and new) seems to be the natural thing for her to do. She also enjoys experimenting with other materials such as plastic bags, coffee bags, and paper.

MATERIALS AND CUTTING INSTRUCTIONS

3 different fabrics for the outer bag (You can use yardage, fat quarters, or scraps from your stash.)

1 fat quarter (18″ × 22″) fabric for the lining

10″ × 12″ cotton batting

Scraps of fabric for the appliqué bird body, wing, and beak

Cream-colored embroidery floss

1 small pearl for the eye

1 sequin for the eye

A few small buttons

7″ zipper

Fusible web

CONSTRUCTION

Pattern is on page 106. All seam allowances are ¼".
Embroidery stitches can be found on page 111.

Make the bag front and back

1. From the 3 fabrics, cut out 3 sections for the front and 3 sections for the back. (Use the template and choose the size of the parts yourself.)

2. Sew together the 3 front and 3 back sections. Press the seams to one side.

Appliqué

1. Trace the appliqué shapes onto the paper backing of the fusible web.

2. With an iron, apply the fusible web to the back of your chosen fabrics. Cut out the shapes, and remove the paper.

3. Press the bird appliqué to the front of the bag, using the project photo for reference.

4. Machine stitch the appliqué to the bag in one continuous line without stopping.

Embellish

1. With cream-colored embroidery floss, add the branch using a chain stitch. Pay attention to the spot where the front and back branches meet at the side of the bag.

2. At the ends of the branches, sew on buttons for leaves or flowers.

FINISH THE BAG

1. Cut out the batting and the lining.

2. Layer front, batting, and lining with right sides facing out. Similarly, layer back, batting, and lining with right sides facing out. Treat each stack as one fabric and sew in the zipper (front + batting + back together, zipper in the middle). Keep the metal stop at the end a little away from the edge so you will have a nice end when you turn the bag.

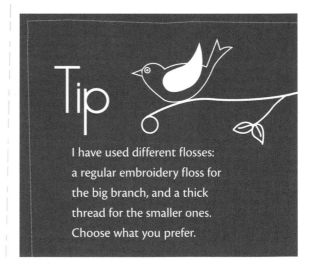

Tip

I have used different flosses: a regular embroidery floss for the big branch, and a thick thread for the smaller ones. Choose what you prefer.

3. Separate the layers, stitch the two lining sides together, and sew together the sides, leaving an opening at the bottom of the lining. Stitch the bag front/batting to the back/batting along sides and bottom. Sew the corners on the lining as well as the front/back pieces. Turn the bag right side out through the lining bottom opening.

4. Stitch the opening in the lining closed. I used a regular stitch to close it with the sewing machine. You can close it with a slip stitch too. Press.

Chewy the Owl Ornament

FINISHED SIZE: 4¼" × 4" × 1"

This peaceful owl will be at home wherever he is hung. The quick assembly using a variety of textures makes gift giving a snap—bet you can't make just one!

ARTIST
Mika Yamamura

EMAIL
info@cuoreco.com

WEBSITES
www.cuore.etsy.com (shop)
www.cuore.typepad.com (blog)

Cuore is inspired by everything from children's fairy tales and vintage movies to modern Japanese design. The line consists of pillows, plushies, pins, tote bags, small accessories, and much more!

A graduate of the Fashion Institute in Los Angeles, Mika Yamamura honed her skills at Paul Frank Industries, where she designed women's accessories for 6½ years.

MATERIALS AND CUTTING INSTRUCTIONS

Patterns are on page 106.

Freezer paper and carbon paper to trace the pattern (If you're fancy, you can scan the patterns onto your computer then print them out onto freezer paper.)

4½" × 9" light gray wool felt for the front and back owl bodies:

- Cut 2 owl bodies.

4" × 2" white vinyl for the owl eyes:

- Cut 2 (1 and 1 reversed) for the left and right eyes.

3" × 1" brown vinyl for the lashes:

- Cut 2 (1 and 1 reversed) for the left and right lashes.

1" × 1" tan vinyl for the beak:

- Cut 1 beak.

3½" × 2½" red wool felt for the belly:

- Cut 1 belly.

4" white rickrack for the belly

8½" ribbon (³⁄₁₆" wide) to hang the owl

Eco-fiberfill for stuffing

CONSTRUCTION

1. Trace all the owl-part patterns onto freezer paper using carbon paper.

2. Using a hot iron, fuse the freezer-paper templates onto each owl body part, and cut out the required number of pieces.

3. Referring to the pattern, position the lashes onto the eye areas, and topstitch using matching brown thread.

4. Position the white eyes onto the front of the owl body, and topstitch using white thread.

5. Topstitch the rickrack onto the center of the owl belly using matching thread.

6. Folding under the ends of the rickrack, position the owl belly on the owl body, and topstitch using red thread.

7. Center the owl beak between the white owl eyes, and topstitch using white thread.

8. Fold the ribbon in half, and position it on the back of the front owl body, using a hot glue gun.

9. Pin the front and back owl bodies together with the wrong sides, and stitch ⅛" from the edge, leaving a 2¼" space at the bottom for stuffing.

10. Stuff the owl body with any kind of fiberfill (I like the eco-fiber kind).

11. Stitch the bottom of the owl body closed.

12. Hang, and enjoy!

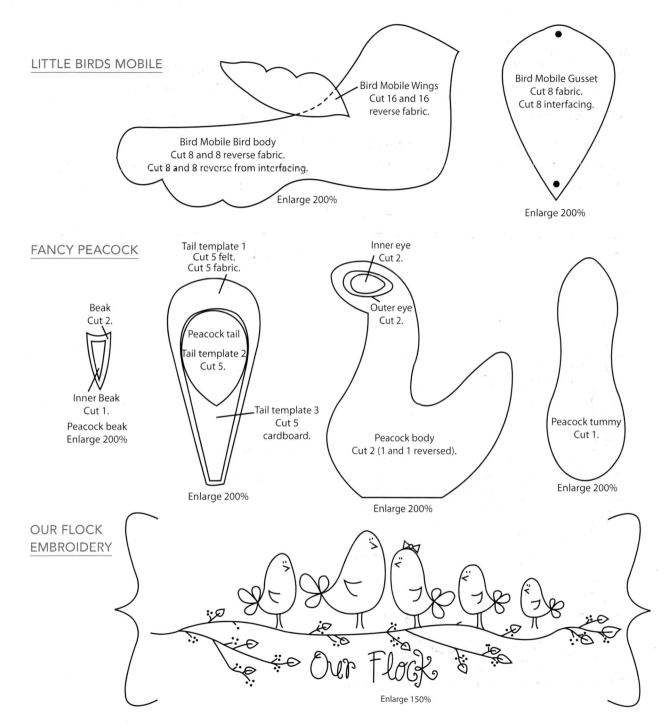

LITTLE BIRDS MOBILE

Bird Mobile Wings
Cut 16 and 16
reverse fabric.

Bird Mobile Bird body
Cut 8 and 8 reverse fabric.
Cut 8 and 8 reverse from interfacing.

Enlarge 200%

Bird Mobile Gusset
Cut 8 fabric.
Cut 8 interfacing.

Enlarge 200%

FANCY PEACOCK

Beak
Cut 2.

Inner Beak
Cut 1.

Peacock beak
Enlarge 200%

Tail template 1
Cut 5 felt.
Cut 5 fabric.

Peacock tail

Tail template 2
Cut 5.

Tail template 3
Cut 5
cardboard.

Enlarge 200%

Inner eye
Cut 2.

Outer eye
Cut 2.

Peacock body
Cut 2 (1 and 1 reversed).

Enlarge 200%

Peacock tummy
Cut 1.

Enlarge 200%

OUR FLOCK EMBROIDERY

Our Flock

Enlarge 150%

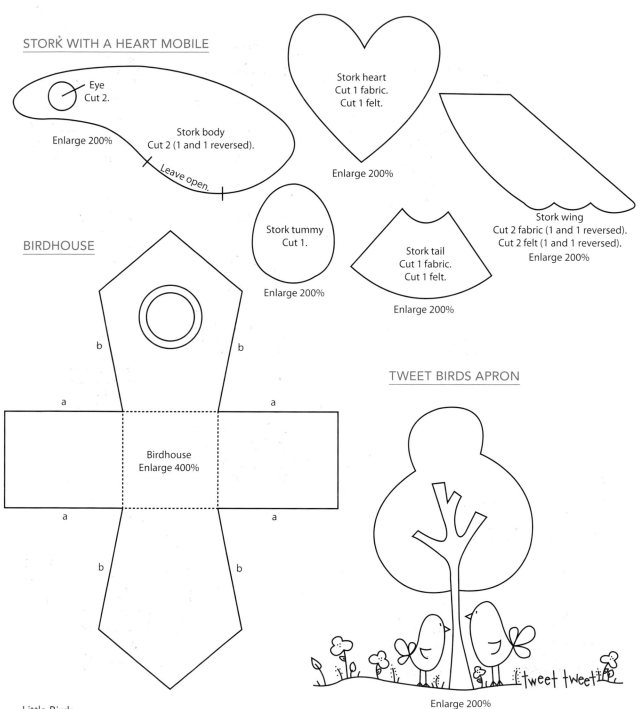

STORK WITH A HEART MOBILE

Eye
Cut 2.

Enlarge 200%

Stork body
Cut 2 (1 and 1 reversed).

Leave open.

Stork heart
Cut 1 fabric.
Cut 1 felt.

Enlarge 200%

Stork wing
Cut 2 fabric (1 and 1 reversed).
Cut 2 felt (1 and 1 reversed).
Enlarge 200%

Stork tummy
Cut 1.

Enlarge 200%

Stork tail
Cut 1 fabric.
Cut 1 felt.

Enlarge 200%

BIRDHOUSE

b   b

a   a

Birdhouse
Enlarge 400%

a   a

b   b

TWEET BIRDS APRON

tweet tweet

Enlarge 200%

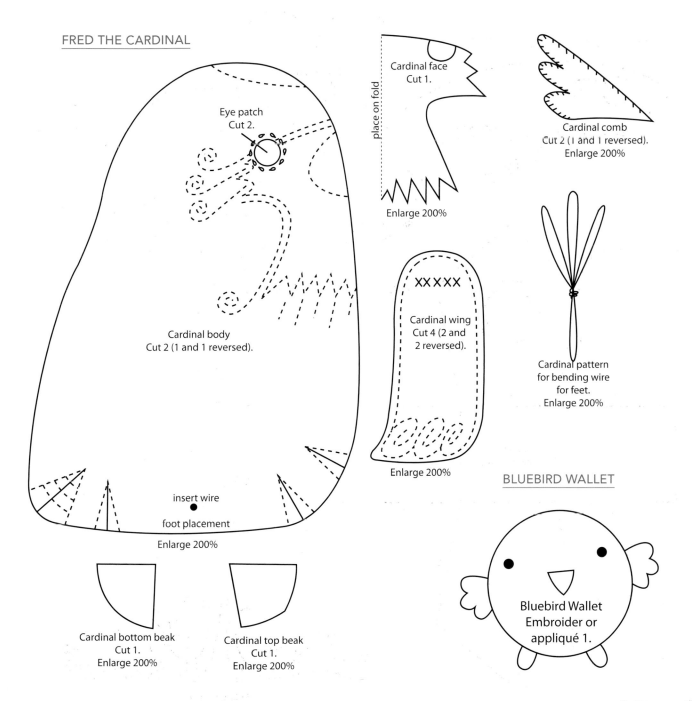

FRED THE CARDINAL

Eye patch
Cut 2.

Cardinal body
Cut 2 (1 and 1 reversed).

insert wire
foot placement
Enlarge 200%

Cardinal bottom beak
Cut 1.
Enlarge 200%

Cardinal top beak
Cut 1.
Enlarge 200%

place on fold

Cardinal face
Cut 1.
Enlarge 200%

Cardinal wing
Cut 4 (2 and
2 reversed).
Enlarge 200%

Cardinal comb
Cut 2 (1 and 1 reversed).
Enlarge 200%

Cardinal pattern
for bending wire
for feet.
Enlarge 200%

BLUEBIRD WALLET

Bluebird Wallet
Embroider or
appliqué 1.

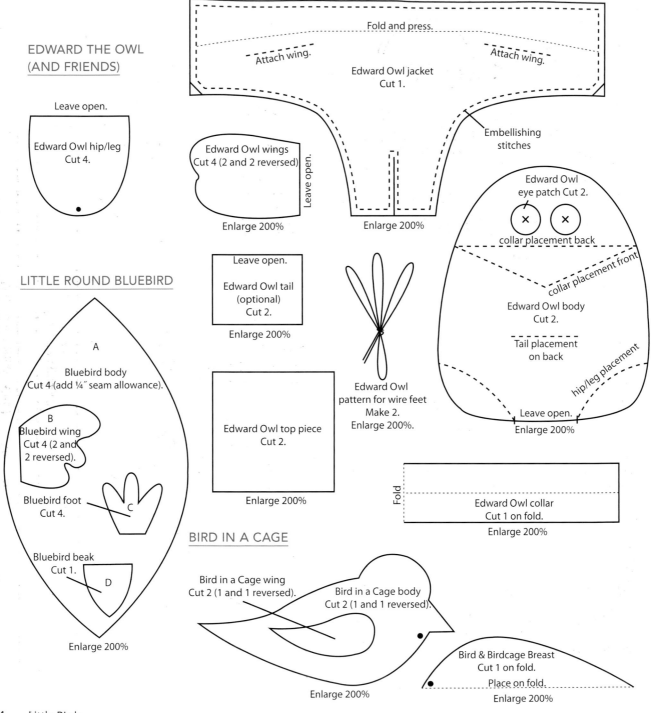

EDWARD THE OWL (AND FRIENDS)

Leave open.

Edward Owl hip/leg
Cut 4.

Fold and press.

Attach wing.

Attach wing.

Edward Owl jacket
Cut 1.

Embellishing
stitches

Edward Owl wings
Cut 4 (2 and 2 reversed)

Leave open.

Enlarge 200%

Enlarge 200%

Edward Owl
eye patch Cut 2.

collar placement back

collar placement front

Edward Owl body
Cut 2.

Tail placement
on back

hip/leg placement

Leave open.

Enlarge 200%

LITTLE ROUND BLUEBIRD

Leave open.

Edward Owl tail
(optional)
Cut 2.

Enlarge 200%

Edward Owl
pattern for wire feet
Make 2.
Enlarge 200%.

A

Bluebird body
Cut 4 (add ¼˝ seam allowance).

B
Bluebird wing
Cut 4 (2 and
2 reversed).

Edward Owl top piece
Cut 2.

Enlarge 200%

Bluebird foot
Cut 4.

C

Bluebird beak
Cut 1.

D

Fold

Edward Owl collar
Cut 1 on fold.

Enlarge 200%

BIRD IN A CAGE

Bird in a Cage wing
Cut 2 (1 and 1 reversed).

Bird in a Cage body
Cut 2 (1 and 1 reversed).

Bird & Birdcage Breast
Cut 1 on fold.

Place on fold.

Enlarge 200%

Enlarge 200%

Enlarge 200%

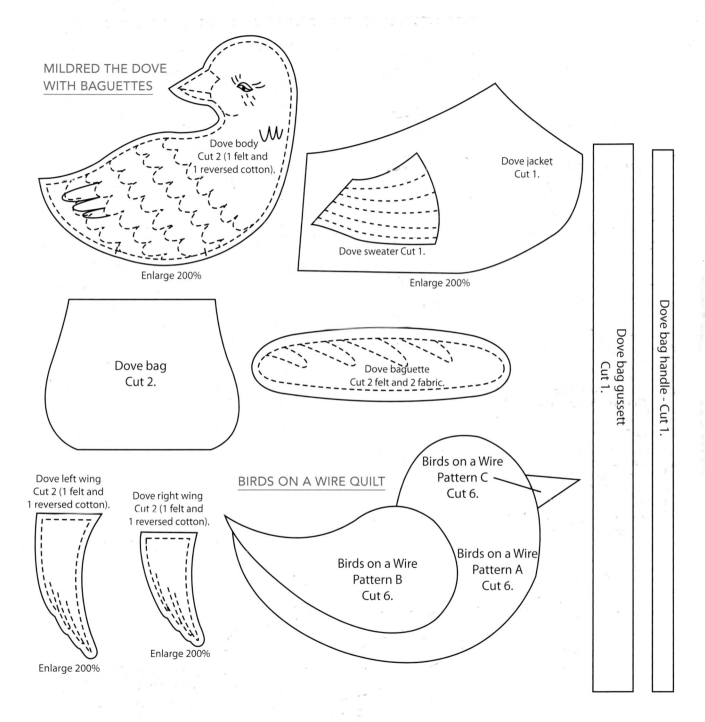

MILDRED THE DOVE
WITH BAGUETTES

Dove body
Cut 2 (1 felt and
1 reversed cotton).

Enlarge 200%

Dove jacket
Cut 1.

Dove sweater Cut 1.

Enlarge 200%

Dove bag
Cut 2.

Dove baguette
Cut 2 felt and 2 fabric.

Dove bag gussett
Cut 1.

Dove bag handle - Cut 1.

Dove left wing
Cut 2 (1 felt and
1 reversed cotton).

Dove right wing
Cut 2 (1 felt and
1 reversed cotton).

Enlarge 200%

Enlarge 200%

BIRDS ON A WIRE QUILT

Birds on a Wire
Pattern C
Cut 6.

Birds on a Wire
Pattern B
Cut 6.

Birds on a Wire
Pattern A
Cut 6.

BIRDS ON A WIRE QUILT

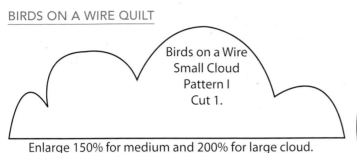

Birds on a Wire
Small Cloud
Pattern I
Cut 1.

Enlarge 150% for medium and 200% for large cloud.

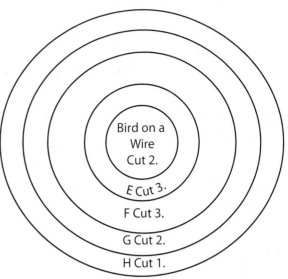

Bird on a
Wire
Cut 2.

E Cut 3.

F Cut 3.

G Cut 2.

H Cut 1.

WREATH WITH A BIRD

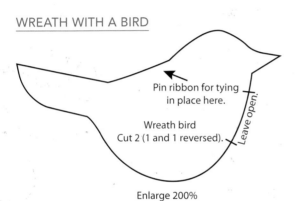

Pin ribbon for tying
in place here.

Wreath bird
Cut 2 (1 and 1 reversed).

Leave open.

Enlarge 200%

CHEWY THE OWL ORNAMENT

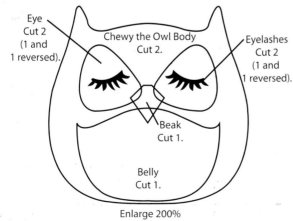

Eye
Cut 2
(1 and
1 reversed).

Chewy the Owl Body
Cut 2.

Eyelashes
Cut 2
(1 and
1 reversed).

Beak
Cut 1.

Belly
Cut 1.

Enlarge 200%

BIRD ON A BRANCH MAKEUP BAG

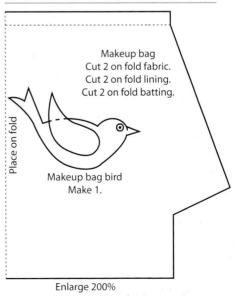

Makeup bag
Cut 2 on fold fabric.
Cut 2 on fold lining.
Cut 2 on fold batting.

Place on fold

Makeup bag bird
Make 1.

Enlarge 200%

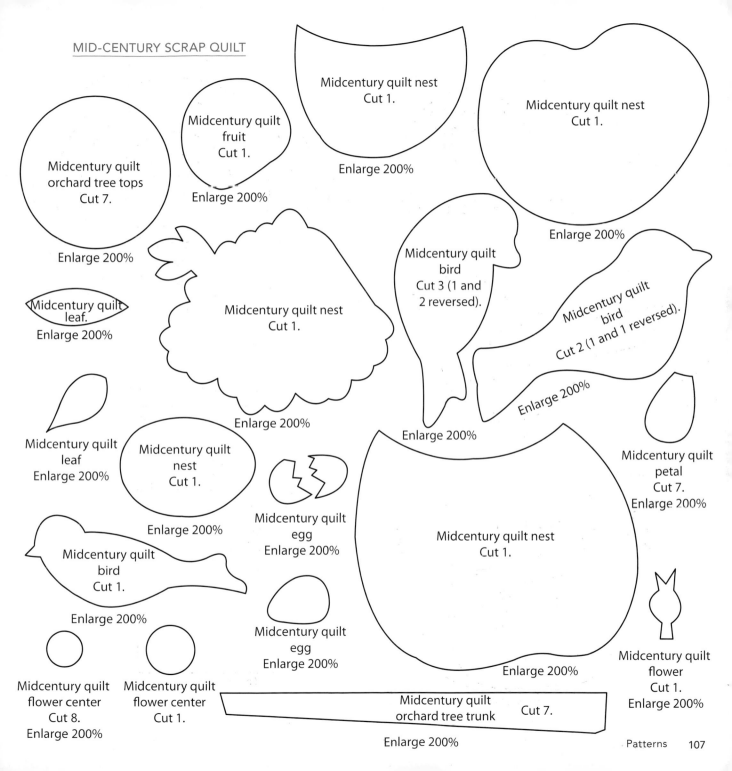

MID-CENTURY SCRAP QUILT

Midcentury quilt
orchard tree tops
Cut 7.
Enlarge 200%

Midcentury quilt
fruit
Cut 1.
Enlarge 200%

Midcentury quilt nest
Cut 1.
Enlarge 200%

Midcentury quilt nest
Cut 1.
Enlarge 200%

Midcentury quilt
leaf.
Enlarge 200%

Midcentury quilt nest
Cut 1.
Enlarge 200%

Midcentury quilt
bird
Cut 3 (1 and
2 reversed).
Enlarge 200%

Midcentury quilt
bird
Cut 2 (1 and 1 reversed).
Enlarge 200%

Midcentury quilt
leaf
Enlarge 200%

Midcentury quilt
nest
Cut 1.
Enlarge 200%

Midcentury quilt
egg
Enlarge 200%

Midcentury quilt nest
Cut 1.

Midcentury quilt
petal
Cut 7.
Enlarge 200%

Midcentury quilt
bird
Cut 1.
Enlarge 200%

Midcentury quilt
egg
Enlarge 200%

Enlarge 200%

Midcentury quilt
flower
Cut 1.
Enlarge 200%

Midcentury quilt
flower center
Cut 8.
Enlarge 200%

Midcentury quilt
flower center
Cut 1.

Midcentury quilt
orchard tree trunk   Cut 7.

Enlarge 200%

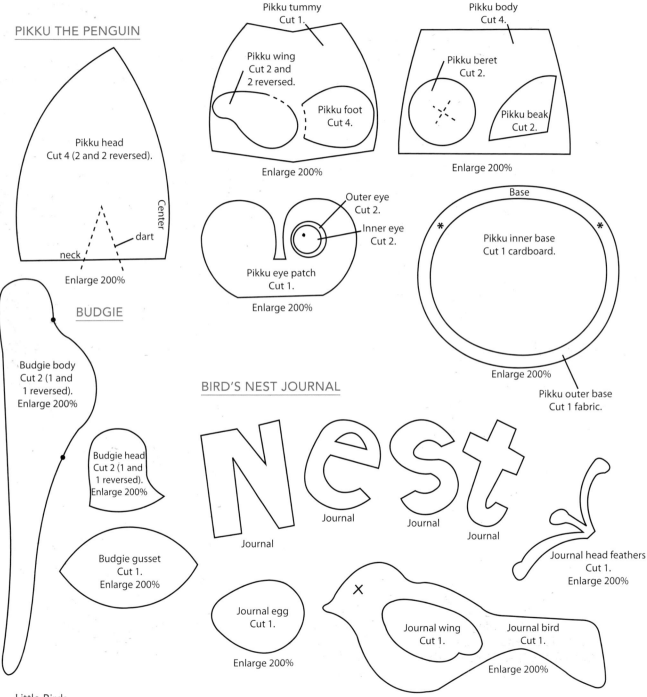

PIKKU THE PENGUIN

Pikku head
Cut 4 (2 and 2 reversed).

Enlarge 200%

neck

dart

Center

Pikku tummy
Cut 1.

Pikku wing
Cut 2 and
2 reversed.

Pikku foot
Cut 4.

Enlarge 200%

Pikku body
Cut 4.

Pikku beret
Cut 2.

Pikku beak
Cut 2.

Enlarge 200%

Outer eye
Cut 2.

Inner eye
Cut 2.

Pikku eye patch
Cut 1.

Enlarge 200%

Base

*

*

Pikku inner base
Cut 1 cardboard.

Enlarge 200%

Pikku outer base
Cut 1 fabric.

BUDGIE

Budgie body
Cut 2 (1 and
1 reversed).
Enlarge 200%

Budgie head
Cut 2 (1 and
1 reversed).
Enlarge 200%

Budgie gusset
Cut 1.
Enlarge 200%

BIRD'S NEST JOURNAL

Nest

Journal

Journal

Journal

Journal

Journal

Journal head feathers
Cut 1.
Enlarge 200%

Journal egg
Cut 1.

Enlarge 200%

Journal wing
Cut 1.

Journal bird
Cut 1.

Enlarge 200%

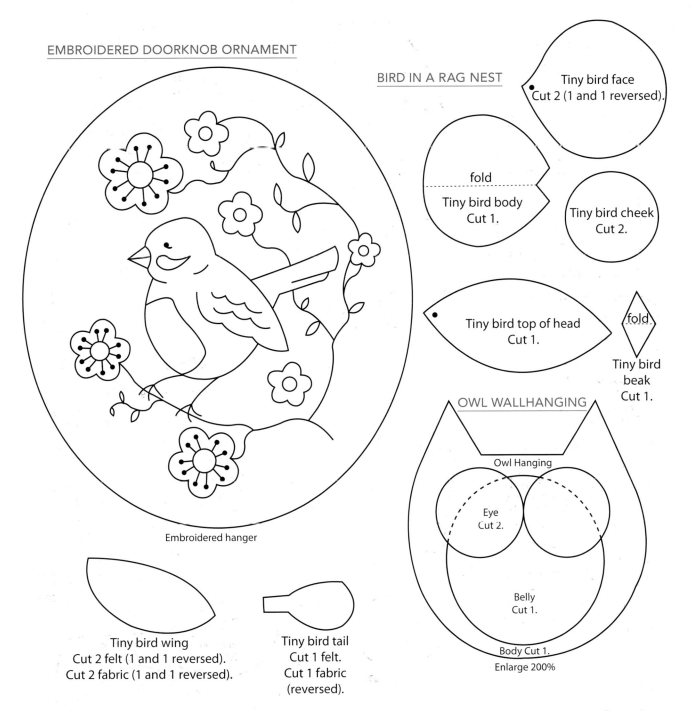

EMBROIDERED DOORKNOB ORNAMENT

Embroidered hanger

Tiny bird wing
Cut 2 felt (1 and 1 reversed).
Cut 2 fabric (1 and 1 reversed).

Tiny bird tail
Cut 1 felt.
Cut 1 fabric
(reversed).

BIRD IN A RAG NEST

Tiny bird face
Cut 2 (1 and 1 reversed).

fold
Tiny bird body
Cut 1.

Tiny bird cheek
Cut 2.

Tiny bird top of head
Cut 1.

fold
Tiny bird
beak
Cut 1.

OWL WALLHANGING

Owl Hanging

Eye
Cut 2.

Belly
Cut 1.

Body Cut 1.
Enlarge 200%

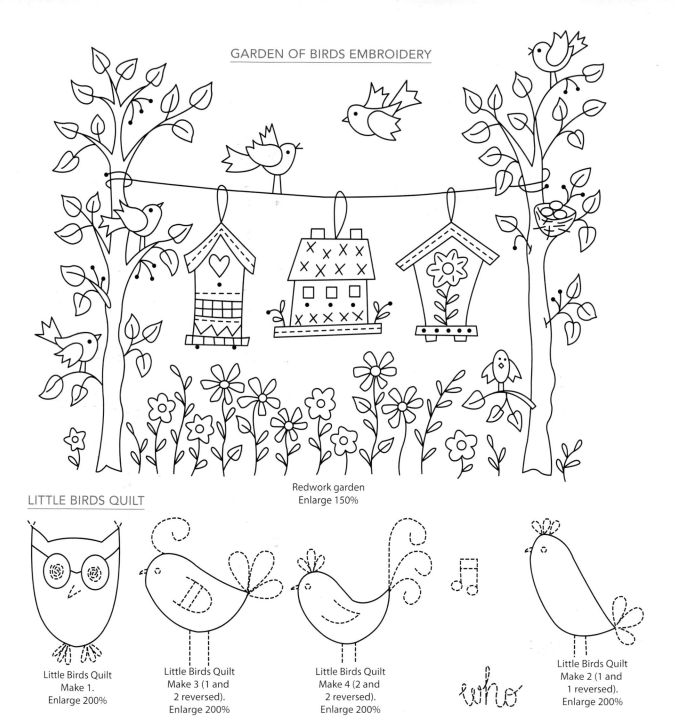

GARDEN OF BIRDS EMBROIDERY

Redwork garden
Enlarge 150%

Little Birds Quilt
Make 1.
Enlarge 200%

Little Birds Quilt
Make 3 (1 and
2 reversed).
Enlarge 200%

Little Birds Quilt
Make 4 (2 and
2 reversed).
Enlarge 200%

Little Birds Quilt
Make 2 (1 and
1 reversed).
Enlarge 200%

EMBROIDERY STITCHES

Backstitch

Blanket/ buttonhole stitch

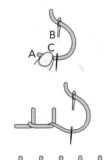

Chain stitch

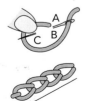

Cross stitch

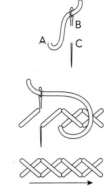

French knot

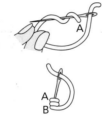

Ladder stitch

Lazy daisy stitch

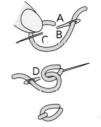

Running stitch

Satin stitch

Split stitch

Stem stitch

Whipstitch

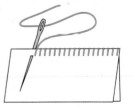

For a list of other fine books from C&T Publishing, ask for a free catalog:

C&T Publishing, Inc.
P.O. Box 1456
Lafayette, CA 94549

800-284-1114

Email: ctinfo@ctpub.com
Website: www.ctpub.com

Tips and Techniques can be found at www.ctpub.com > Consumer Resources > Quiltmaking Basics: Tips & Techniques for Quiltmaking & More

C&T Publishing's professional photography services are now available to the public. Visit us at www.ctmediaservices.com.

FOR QUILTING SUPPLIES:
Cotton Patch
1025 Brown Ave.
Lafayette, CA 94549

Store: 925-284-1177
Mail order: 925-283-7883

Email: CottonPa@aol.com
Website: www.quiltusa.com

NOTE: Fabrics used in the quilts and projects shown may not be currently available, as fabric manufacturers keep most fabrics in print for only a short time.

C&T would like to thank Michael Miller Fabrics for the generous supplying of Lantern Bloom Collection by Laura Gunn used in many of the photographs.